BOOK OF ANSWERS

ARIZONA-SONORA DESERT MUSEUM

BOOK OF ANSWERS

BY DAVID WENTWORTH LAZAROFF

ARIZONA-SONORA DESERT MUSEUM PRESS

Copyright © 1998 by
Arizona-Sonora Desert Museum

All rights reserved.

Published in the United States by Arizona-Sonora
Desert Museum, 2021 North Kinney Road,
Tucson, Arizona 85743
www.desert.net/museum

This book is available at quantity discounts
for educational, business, or sales promotional
use. For further information, please contact
Arizona-Sonora Desert Museum Press, 2021
North Kinney Road, Tucson, Arizona 85743
(520) 883-3028

Library of Congress Cataloging-in-Publication Data

Lazaroff, David Wentworth, 1948-
        Arizona-Sonora Desert Museum book of
answers / by David Wentworth Lazaroff.
        p. cm.
    Includes bibliographical references (p.   ) and
index.
    ISBN 1-886679-09-6
    1. Deserts — Miscellanea. 2. Desert Plants —
Miscellanea. 3. Desert Animals — Miscellanea.
4. Sonoran Desert — Miscellanea.
    I. Arizona-Sonora Desert Museum (Tucson, Ariz.)
II. Title.
QH88.L39 1998
578.754—dc21   97-31829
                           CIP

Project Coordinator:
  Steven J. Phillips

Book Design:
  Larry Lindahl Design

Cover Design:
  Steven J. Phillips and Larry Lindahl

Photography (front cover and pages i-4):
  Saguaro cactus—Jim Honcoop
  Costa's hummingbird—ASDM photo by James Flynn
  Giant swallowtail butterfly—Jim Honcoop
  Giant hairy scorpion—ASDM photo by Paul and
    Shirley Berquist
  Javelina—ASDM photo by Rico Leffanta
  Rainbow cactus in bloom—Jim Honcoop

Illustrations:
  Pamela Ensign 13, 18, 19, 32, 36, 37, 38, 43,
  44, 46, 48, 51, 52, 53, 58, 59, 60, 62, 63, 70,
  73, 74, 82, 85, 87, 91, 93, 94, 98, 103, 104,
  106, 117, 120, 123, 192, back cover

Additional Illustrations:
  Randy Babb 14, 76, 77, 78, 80, 108, 112, 115
  Lucretia Breazeale Hamilton 23
  Jonathan Hanson 21
  Jeffrey Martin 31, 65, 66, 86
  Linda Meyer 97
  Paul Mirocha 27
  Narca Moore-Craig 96, 99, 126, 128
  Deborah Reade 2, 9, 10, 16
  Rachel Taylor 29, 56
  Nicholas Wilson 7, 109
  Vera Ming Wong 54

CONTENTS

PREFACE

I WISH I COULD SAY this book was my idea, but it wasn't. It was the inspiration of the Arizona-Sonora Desert Museum's Publications Manager, Steve Phillips.

A few years ago Steve was a newcomer to the Sonoran Desert, and like every new arrival since time immemorial, he was receiving an eye-opening introduction not only to the desert's many delights, but also to its heat, scorpions, and caliche. How to deal with these things? And why on earth is it like this?

Steve was unusually fortunate: he had the entire staff of the Desert Museum to consult. He also realized that a collection of answers to the sorts of questions he had would be helpful to anyone living in the Sonoran Desert, newcomer or not, and he offered the job of writing the book to me.

We began by polling the Desert Museum staff to discover what questions they were most frequently asked. The responses were revealing.

Some questions simply reflected the realities of life on the Museum grounds. "Where's the restaurant?" and "Where are the restrooms?" were on the list, of course, but I hadn't expected the bewildered "Where are the monkeys and elephants?"

Other questions showed the staff having fun with our poll. A typical example: "Do hummingbirds really migrate on the backs of geese? Uncle Mike says so. He's seen it."[1] Another: "In order to cook a dog, how long should you leave it in your car in June?"[2] And my personal favorite: "Are javelina rodents? Pigs? What are those suckers?" (Soberly reworded, that one made the final cut.)

But, despite the levity, most of the questions submitted by the staff were thoughtfully chosen, and by stages they were winnowed, merged, and refined into the forty-two in this book. I hope you'll find the answers useful, and interesting, too.

Many people gave generously of their time, information, and hard-won experience to help create this publication and to rescue me from error. I've listed them below. To everyone who helped, my sincere thanks.

Arizona-Sonora Desert Museum, especially Carol Cochran, Mark Dimmitt, Rich Dulaney, Craig Ivanyi, Nancy Laney, Renée Lizotte, Axhel Muñoz, Gary Nabhan, Steve Phillips, Bob Scarborough, Peter Siminski, Barbara Terkanian, Tom Van Devender, Docents Linda Gregonis and William M. Taylor, and volunteers Mary Chris Carbonaro, Gloria Montejo Ferrell, and Timothy Tilton, Arizona-Sonora Desert Museum; Cynthia J. Anderson and Kathi Bonnell, Central Arizona Chapter, and Jane Cripps, Southern Arizona Chapter, American Red Cross; Janet L. Jacobsen, *Arizona Great Outdoors*; Jerry Feldner, Arizona Herpetological Association; Arizona-Sonora Desert Museum Gift Shops; Scott Richardson, Sandy Cate, and Jeff Howland, Arizona Game and Fish Department; Jude McNally, Arizona Poison and Drug Information Center; Steve Thoenes, BeeMaster, Inc.; The Book Mark; Bob Parker, Bureau of Land Management, Ridgecrest Research Area, California Desert District; Frank Hoover, California Department of Fish and Game; Stephen L. Buchmann and Justin O. Schmidt, Carl Hayden Bee Research Center, USDA Agricultural Research Service; Centers for Disease Control and Prevention, U.S. Department of Health and Human Services; Coronado National Forest; Dave Vaughn, Dave's Antique Service; David Pfennig, Department of Biology, University of North Carolina, Chapel Hill; George Bradley, Peter Holm, Robert McCord, Yar Petryszyn, and Philip Rosen, Department of Ecology and Evolutionary Biology, University of Arizona; Carl Olson, Department of Entomology, University of Arizona; Donald F. Post, Department of Soil, Water, and Environmental Science, University of Arizona; Lisa Shubitz, D.V.M., Department of Veterinary Science, University of Arizona; Joseph R. McAuliffe, Desert Botanical Garden; Kern Medical Center; Ruth Kneale; Rex Adams, Christopher Baisan, and Alex McCord, Laboratory of Tree Ring Research, University of Arizona; Janet and Lewis Miller, licensed wildlife rehabilitators; National Outdoor Leadership School; Anne Fletcher, The Living Desert Wildlife and Botanical Park; Darren McCollum, National Weather Service; Office of Climatology, Arizona State University; Babs Johnson and Elizabeth MacNeil, MD, MPH, Pima County Health Department; Steve Anderson, Pima County Parks and Recreation; William K. Hartmann, Planetary Science Institute; Carla Danforth, Judy Edison, Cherie Lazaroff, and Carol de Waard, Tucson Audubon Society and the Audubon Nature Shop; Todd Esque, U.S. Geological Survey, Biological Resources Division; Cecil Schwalbe, U.S. Geological Survey, Cooperative Park Studies Unit, University of Arizona; John N. Galgiani, M.D., and Margaret Kurzius-Spencer, Valley Fever Center for Excellence; Barbara Tellman, Water Resources Research Center, University of Arizona; Gregory D. McCurdy, Western Regional Climate Center, Desert Research Institute.

1. Absolutely not. Is this the same Uncle Mike who was abducted by aliens?

2. It depends on the time of day, the size of the dog, and the degree of doneness desired.

INTRODUCTION

THIS IS A BOOK of answers to questions about the Sonoran Desert. You might think of it as a sort of manual for living in that sunny quarter of the American Southwest. It's not a complete manual, by any means: it won't help you season a *burrito* or service your evaporative cooler! But it will help you enjoy and live peaceably with the Sonoran Desert's unusual natural world.

Newcomers should find this book especially useful, but it isn't just a beginner's manual. The questions in these pages are some of those most frequently posed to the staff of the Arizona-Sonora Desert Museum, and many of those doing the asking are long-time desert dwellers who've recently encountered something new.

That's part of the fun of living in the Sonoran Desert. It never stops surprising you!

AREA COVERED BY THIS BOOK

The Sonoran Desert is a big place—about 100,000 square miles, if you like statistics—large enough to vary a great deal from south to north and west to east. As you can see on the map on the next page, much of the Sonoran Desert lies in Mexico (partly in the state of Sonora,

from which it gets its name). This book is concerned only with the part of the Sonoran Desert in the United States. This includes portions of two of the desert's six subdivisions.

The *Lower Colorado River Valley* is the Sonoran Desert's hottest and driest subdivision. It includes not only the actual valley of the lower Colorado but also areas far to its west and east in California and Arizona. It's a region of broad, flat valleys dotted with widely spaced creosote bushes, interrupted by low mountain ranges and occasional fields of sand dunes.

The *Arizona Upland* is the Sonoran Desert's coolest subdivision—it has fairly frequent winter frosts—and it forms the desert's northeastern border. It has taller mountains, narrower valleys, and greater rainfall than the Lower Colorado River Valley, and much of its vegetation is more varied and lush, with many cacti and small trees.

HOW TO USE THIS BOOK

It's easy! First, let's look at how it's organized.

There are forty-two questions (and answers), divided among the book's three sections. Section 1, "Getting to Know

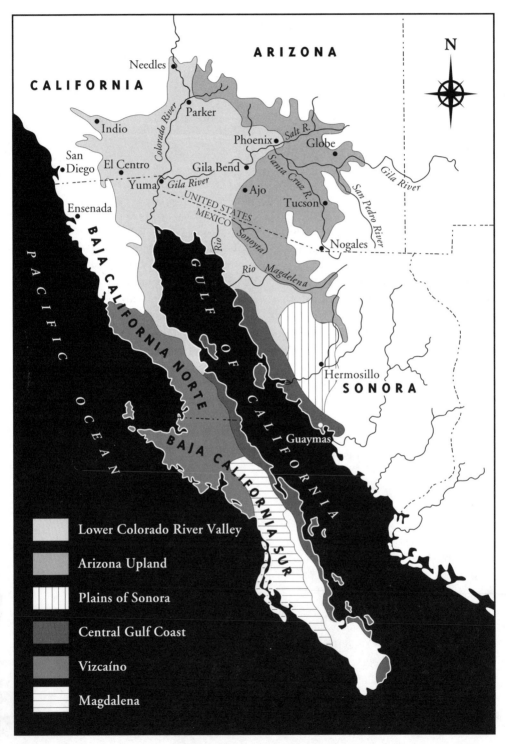

The six subdivisions of the Sonoran Desert

the Desert," introduces some basic facts about the Sonoran Desert. Section 2, "Around the Home," gives tips on desert houses and gardens. Section 3, "Enjoying the Outdoors," offers advice about hiking and driving in the desert.

After the questions there are several appendixes with in-depth information about special topics, such as the climate and bites and stings. The last appendix helps you find information from other sources. (We'll get to that in a moment.) The book ends with a bibliography, a list of organizations, a glossary, and an index.

Of course, you can get started in the usual ways, by just browsing or by consulting the table of contents or the index. Once you begin reading the answer to a question, you'll find some navigational aids. Notes in the text make connections to other questions and to the appendixes. There's also a list of cross-references at the end of each answer. Unusual or technical terms are in **bold** and defined in the glossary.

If after exploring all the cross-references you still want to find out more, it will be time to visit Appendix G: Additional Sources. Codes in this appendix will point you to helpful books and organizations in the two lists that follow it.

IS THERE A MESSAGE?

There's no moral on the last page of this book, but you may notice two themes running through the answers to the questions.

The first is this: you'll find living in the Sonoran Desert easiest and most satisfying if you simply accept the desert as it is. There's really very little to fear in this place, and a great deal of pleasure in feeling truly at home in a land that's hot and dry.

And the second theme: the Sonoran Desert is a wonderful place! Not only is it strikingly beautiful and endlessly varied, but the more you learn about it, the more fascinating it becomes. We are very lucky to live here.

We believe you'll find many uses for this book, but we hope that after reading it you won't feel like dropping it on the tarantula that shows up in the kitchen. We hope that instead you'll take a minute to get acquainted with your interesting visitor, and then use this volume to shoo it gently out the door.

Getting to Know the Desert

THE SONORAN DESERT takes some getting used to. It's a place where "rivers" have no water; where plants are so spiny you don't dare reach out to catch your fall; where summer is interminable but winter passes in an eye-blink; where pigs aren't pigs; where toads spring miraculously from rain-pounded soil; where landscapes are pastels but sunsets are beyond Kodachrome; and where people splash in swimming pools near dried-out lawns painted green.

Yet, believe it or not, this exotic place can seem just as natural and logical as anywhere else—once you get to know it. These first few questions should help you make sense of it all.

QUESTION 1

What exactly is a desert?

ANSWER: *A place where lack of water is severely limiting to living things most of the time.*

Depending on who's counting, there are about twenty major deserts on our planet, each a unique and fascinating world in itself, and it's no easy task to find one description that fits them all. The deceptively simple definition above is as good as any, and it has much to say about what a desert is. But let's start with what it *doesn't* say.

First, it says nothing about what a desert looks like. For many of us, the word "desert" calls to mind expanses of sun-baked sand dunes, but the world's deserts also encompass barren salt flats, snow-swept plateaus, fog-cloaked coastal plains, cactus-studded mountains, and a great many other distinctive and beautiful landscapes besides.

Second, and perhaps more surprisingly, the definition says nothing about heat. Freezing temperatures are actually commonplace in many deserts, especially those far from the equator and the ameliorating effects of oceans—for example the deserts of Central Asia and our own Great Basin Desert. At the chilliest extreme are the polar deserts of Antarctica and Greenland, where the frigid air can hold scant moisture, and what little precipitation there is comes in frozen form.

So what *do* all deserts have in common? The definition has the answer: aridity. A desert is a dry place, not necessarily a hot one (though heat is one way to make a desert dry). It's a place where plants, animals, and human beings have adapted to—even thrive

PET THEORIES

Aridity is often measured by comparing precipitation to **evapotranspiration**—the combination of evaporation directly from the soil and **transpiration** from the leaves and stems of plants. In the world's drier places more water could theoretically be lost every year by evapotranspiration than is actually delivered as rain and snow, so we have to speak in terms of *potential* evapotranspiration, or PET for short. One simple way to classify climates is by the ratio of PET to precipitation—the so-called PET ratio.

Some say a PET ratio greater than 2:1 is a sure recipe for a desert. Yet the plant community near the Desert Museum is so lush some ecologists say it's not desert vegetation at all, but **thornscrub**—despite a PET ratio of about 8:1. Yuma, Arizona, in the Sonoran Desert's most arid core, has a PET ratio of about 50:1. But even this—true desert by almost anyone's standards—pales by comparison to parts of the Sahara, which have PET ratios greater than 1000:1!

precipitation but also losses by evaporation, in order to gauge the soil moisture available to plants. All agree that wherever much more moisture could theoretically be evaporated from the soil than is actually delivered by precipitation, a desert will result. Exactly *how much* more is a matter for debate. (See sidebar, this page.)

From the standpoint of our definition, though, what matters isn't how we measure dryness but its effects on living things. In deserts the forms and life cycles of many plants and animals show striking adaptations to aridity—succulents hoarding water against drought, dwarf trees shedding their leaves between rains, and nocturnal rodents living on the moisture produced by their own metabolism (to list just a few). And because water scarcity severely limits the vegetation the land can support, desert landscapes are usually open and uncrowded. In fact, this is one of the very few ways almost all deserts look alike.

In the end even the most elaborate definition can tell us only so much about what a desert truly is. The best way to find that out is to experience a desert yourself.

Related questions:

Q2. Why is the Sonoran Desert so hot and dry?
Q3. Are there seasons in the Sonoran Desert?
Q13. Do I need to water native desert plants? (sidebar, page 45)
Q32. If I run out of water in the desert can I get some from a barrel cactus? (sidebar, page 98)
Q34. Why don't I see very many animals when I hike in the desert?

in—an environment where water is usually scarce and its arrival almost always unpredictable.

♦ How dry must a place be to be called a desert?

Ecologists and geographers have made many attempts to define deserts (and other **biomes**) by their climates. Most recent efforts take into account not only

QUESTION

Why is the Sonoran Desert so hot and dry?

ANSWER: *Mostly because of its latitude.*

Of course, that's just a simple way to sum up a very complicated situation. To see how it all works, let's take the two parts of this question in turn.

◆ *Why is the Sonoran Desert so hot?*

No mystery here. The Sonoran Desert dips a toe into the tropics at the tip of Baja California, reaching south of the Tropic of Cancer nearly to latitude 23°. Its northern limit is at about 35°, near Needles, California. At these latitudes the sun passes nearly overhead at noon in June and July. The sun heats the ground, the ground heats the air, and the air heats the meteorologists' thermometers.

It also helps that most of the region is at low elevations. The lowest areas tend to be the hottest. That's why Yuma, in the Lower Colorado River Valley subdivision of the Sonoran Desert, is usually

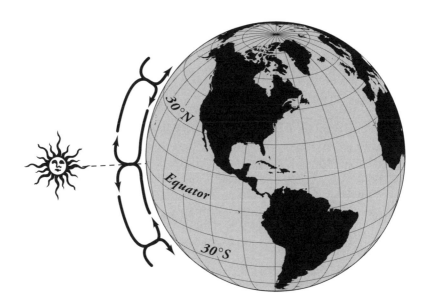

Atmospheric circulation in the tropics and subtropics in spring and fall.

RAIN SHADOWS

Some of the same desert-making processes at work in the Earth's grand atmospheric circulation patterns happen in miniature around mountain ranges. Wet air moving up windward mountain slopes expands and cools, clouds form, and the moisture falls out as rain or snow. By the time the air descends the leeward slopes (contracting and reheating as it goes) it has been drained of

moisture. As a result, lands downwind of mountain ranges tend to be dry; we say they lie in a **rain shadow.**

Much of the Sonoran Desert in the United States is dry partly because it lies in a *double* rain shadow. In winter mountains in southern California wring moisture from air approaching from the Pacific Ocean. In summer the Mexican Sierra Madres do the same to air on its way from the Gulf of Mexico.

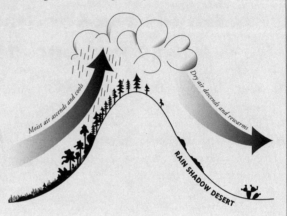

Moist air ascends and cools

Dry air descends and rewarms

RAIN SHADOW DESERT

considerably warmer than Tucson, in the Arizona Upland. (See map, page 2).

◆ Why is the Sonoran Desert so dry?

It's dry partly because high temperatures evaporate the little rainfall it gets. Why it gets so little in the first place is more complicated. It may help first to recall some fundamentals about air.

1. When air is heated it rises.

2. When air rises it expands and cools. (Physicists call this "adiabatic cooling.")

3. When air cools it can hold less moisture. What it can no longer hold condenses and forms clouds, raindrops, hailstones, or snowflakes.

Here's how all this applies to the Sonoran Desert. Warm, wet air near the equator rises, cools, and drops its moisture in heavy rains. (That's why there are tropical rainforests.) By the time it reaches

high altitudes it's cold and dry, and when it can rise no farther it spreads out and moves toward the poles. Then, near about 30° north and south (the **horse latitudes**), it begins to sink towards the earth's surface.

Now adiabatic cooling works in reverse. The falling air compresses and heats up. When it reaches the ground it's both hot and dry. Not only does it contribute almost no moisture, it steals it from soils, plants, and animals alike. Meanwhile, the sinking air creates a zone of high pressure from which it spills outward across the land, preventing moister air from reaching the area from elsewhere. The result: a desert.

This is a planet-wide circulation pattern, and because of it the world's hot deserts, including the Sonoran, lie in two broad bands centered roughly 30° north and south of the equator. For this reason they're often called "horse latitude deserts" or "subtropical deserts."

• So why isn't Georgia a desert?

Local conditions often complicate matters in the subtropics (and everywhere else). In the summer, hot air spilling out of the high pressure belt over the Atlantic picks up so much moisture that it's extremely humid when it reaches the southeastern United States. So Georgians enjoy the company of alligators instead of Gila monsters.

• Doesn't it ever rain in the Sonoran Desert?

If the sun were always parked over the equator perhaps it never would! But because of the tilt of the Earth's axis the sun is directly above the equator only in March and September. As the sun moves north and south during the rest of the year it tends to drag the atmosphere's circulation patterns along with it.

In winter the entire system shifts south with the sun. The zone of sinking air and high pressure moves out of the way, allowing westerly winds to import moisture from the northern Pacific. It's delivered mostly in the form of gentle, widespread rainstorms.

In summer the whole circulation system follows the sun north. At the same time, intense solar heating causes the air over the desert to rise, creating low pressure near the ground that overwhelms the subtropical high pressure zone and sucks in moist air from the Sea of Cortez. These **monsoon** winds result in violent localized thunderstorms. (Much less moisture reaches the desert from the more distant Gulf of Mexico.

See sidebar, previous page.) In late summer tropical hurricane remnants called **chubascos** sometimes bring more widespread rains.

> *A climatological rule of thumb: the less the rainfall in an area, the more variable it is. Deserts aren't only the driest places on earth; they're also the places where precipitation varies most dramatically from year to year. It's not enough for desert animals and plants to be adapted to the averages; they must be prepared for the extremes—to exploit the extra-wet times and survive the extra-dry.*

Winter and summer rains don't reach all parts of the Sonoran Desert equally. Areas west of the Colorado River receive almost all their rain in the winter; they seldom have summer storms. Eastward (farther from the Pacific) the winter rains gradually diminish, but increasing summer rains more than compensate. Tucson, near the desert's eastern edge, receives about equal portions of rain in the summer and winter, and about three times as much overall as Yuma.

Related questions:

Q1. What exactly is a desert?
Q3. Are there seasons in the Sonoran Desert?
See also Appendix A: Climate.

Are there seasons in the Sonoran Desert?

ANSWER: *Yes, but they're quite different from the seasons in temperate climates.*

So different, in fact, that naturalists don't all agree on what to call them, when they begin and end, or even how many there are! The situation is complicated by the unpredictability of desert rainfall, which profoundly affects both the timing and the character of every season. The Desert Museum recognizes five seasons in its surroundings in the Arizona Upland. How many do you count?

SPRING

FEBRUARY TO APRIL. A time for desert wildflowers, but the picture-postcard displays happen only if fall and winter rains have been just right. Rainfall during the spring itself is usually sporadic, and the flowers race to bloom as days warm and the soil dries: first delicate **annuals**, then **perennials** and small shrubs, finally mesquites and most cacti. A few birds, like mourning doves and curve-billed thrashers, begin nesting as the season opens, others

Brittlebush

join in as the weeks pass, and some mammals, coyotes and cottontails for example, bear young as well.

FORESUMMER or DRY SUMMER

MAY AND JUNE. Foresummer is like winter turned on its head: the most difficult period for many desert animals and plants isn't the coldest, it's the hottest. Annuals have dropped their seeds and dried out, many perennials are dormant (some leafless), and some small mammals are inactive, too, **estivating** until wet weather returns. But not all is quiet—except perhaps during the heat of midday. Paloverdes, ironwoods, and saguaros bloom, birds continue nesting, lizards forage in the morning and evening, and javelina move about in the cool of the night.

SUMMER MONSOON

JULY TO MID-SEPTEMBER. The humid **monsoon** season begins with a thunderclap and the scent of rain. Thunderstorms bring momentarily milder temperatures, flash floods in the arroyos,

A SECOND OPINION

Describing the Sonoran Desert's climate in terms of the familiar cycle of spring, summer, fall, and winter is a bit of a stretch. Perhaps we need a new vocabulary to free us from associations with words coined in far away, cooler places. Here's how the Tohono O'odham Indians divide up the desert year, which begins for them at the very peak of heat and drought.

Saguaro Moon
June (saguaro fruit is gathered)

Rainy Moon
July

Short Planting Moon
August (late crops are planted)

Dry Grass Moon
September

Small Rains Moon
October

Pleasant Cold Moon
November

Big Cold Moon
December

No More Fat Moon
January (animals lose their fat)

Gray Moon
February

Green Moon
March (plants leaf out)

Yellow Moon
April (the desert blooms)

Painful Moon
May (food is scarce)

For more about the Tohono O'odham, see Question 12.

and so much moisture that life seems to burst from the soil. A second crop of annual wildflowers (different from the spring annuals) appears alongside seedlings of paloverdes and saguaros. As insects emerge, toads dig their way out to breed in arroyos and ephemeral ponds. This is the season of greatest growth for most perennial plants, and a time of renewed nesting for some birds. Paloverdes releaf, mesquites bloom a second time, and cottontails breed again, too.

FALL

MID-SEPTEMBER TO NOVEMBER. Early fall is much like a second dry summer, though conditions are usually less extreme than back in June. The summer bloom fades (in some years to be revived by late rains from an errant tropical storm), most

Harris' antelope squirrel

birds cease breeding, and the summer visitors fly south. Gradually the weather cools, by late October enough to send the lizards back underground. If the winter rains begin in November, seedlings of next spring's wildflowers quickly sprout.

WINTER

DECEMBER AND JANUARY. Gentle rains intermittently moisten the soil, coaxing the annual plants toward the spring.

Meanwhile, trees, cacti, and most other perennial plants have ceased growing (or nearly so) and some small mammals are in **hibernation.** Days are usually mild, but occasionally temperatures drop to freezing during a cloudless night. Once in a while, especially in the higher elevations, snow dusts the desert then quickly melts when the sun shows itself.

• *Are the seasons different in other parts of the Sonoran Desert?*

Warm temperatures come earlier to the Lower Colorado River Valley than to the Arizona Upland, and some living things begin their reproduction and growth earlier as well. The monsoon seldom reaches west of the Colorado River, so the dry summer there often extends nearly unbroken into fall, without the burst of life that attends the thunderstorms farther east. (Other subdivisions of the Sonoran Desert have different climates, too, but they're beyond the scope of this book.)

Related questions:

Q1. What exactly is a desert?
Q2. Why is the Sonoran Desert so hot and dry?
See also Appendix A: Climate

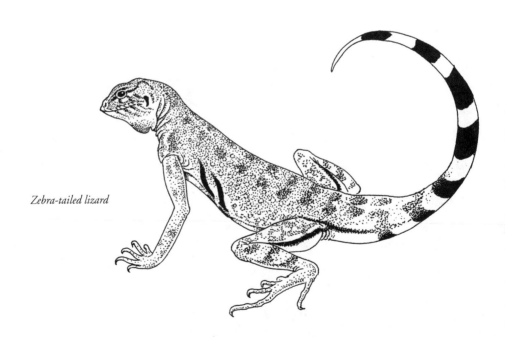

Zebra-tailed lizard

QUESTION 4

Why are sunsets so spectacular in the Sonoran Desert?

ANSWER: *Because the desert air is so clear.*

Even the purest outdoor air teems with tiny floating liquid droplets and solid particles called **aerosols,** and they can affect the appearance of the sky at every time of day. When the aerosols are extremely small we're seldom aware of them (though they have some interesting effects—more on that later). It's when the aerosols are larger that we begin to notice. Then sunlight bouncing off the particles and droplets—a process called **scattering**—makes the sky look hazy. The haze obscures distant objects, turns the midday sky milky white, and dims the light of the setting sun.

Sonoran Desert skies are so often haze-free partly because the air is so dry. In more humid climates water vapor condenses on tiny dust and chemical particles, forming droplets large enough to be seen as hazes and fogs. This is especially true near seacoasts, where airborne salt crystals formed from ocean spray are exceptionally good moisture collectors.

People create hazes, too, mostly by combustion in factories, automobiles, and fireplaces. The Sonoran Desert has relatively few man-caused hazes partly because its population density is still fairly

low. But as towns, cities, and industrial centers grow, this could change. As with so many things that make the desert interesting and beautiful, even the future of its sunsets depends on us.

◆ *Why are sunsets red?*

Oddly enough, the setting sun is red for the same reason the sky is blue!

That reason is **Rayleigh scattering:** the weak scattering of light not by floating particles, but by molecules of the air itself.

While most hues of living things are created by reflection of light off colored pigments, blue eyes and bluebird feathers get their colors from the scattering of light by tiny particles—a process similar to the one that makes the sky blue.

Recall that ordinary white sunlight is a mixture of all the colors (wavelengths) of the visible spectrum, from red and orange

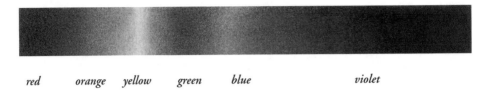

red   orange   yellow   green   blue   violet

The visible spectrum. Light from violet end of the spectrum is much more strongly scattered by air molecules than light from the red end.

at one end to blue and violet at the other. (See diagram above.) Most large aerosols scatter light of all the colors about equally—that's why hazes and fogs look whitish. Air molecules scatter light much differently. Light from the blue-violet end of the spectrum tends to bounce off them, but light from the red-orange end mostly just passes them by.

Imagine looking up into the clear desert sky at midday. What you see is light that has been scattered by air molecules. And since that light comes mostly from the blue-violet end of the spectrum, the sky looks blue.

Now imagine looking at the setting sun. Now its light must take a much longer route through the atmosphere to you. (See diagram below.) By the time it

reaches your eyes so much of the violet, blue, and even green light has been bounced away by air molecules that mostly yellow, orange, and red light is left. The beautiful result: a fiery desert sunset!

◆ So why aren't desert sunrises as red as desert sunsets?

This is where the smallest aerosol particles come in. The tiniest aerosols—mostly too small to be seen as hazes—act much the same way as air molecules: they scatter blue and violet light much more strongly than red and orange. They help make the sky blue and the sunset red.

During the day, breezes and **dust devils** lift very tiny dust particles into the air,

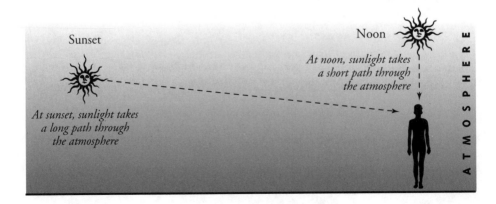

Sunset

At sunset, sunlight takes a long path through the atmosphere

Noon

At noon, sunlight takes a short path through the atmosphere

ATMOSPHERE

and they help to redden the setting sun. Then during the calmer night the dust settles out, so the sunrise is just a pale pink. Of course nature is seldom quite this simple. A lot depends on the weather and the time of year.

♦ *What time of year are the best desert sunsets?*

Every Sonoran Desert season has its own varieties of sunsets. Some say the most beautiful are the subtle clear twilights of spring or fall. But for sheer garish jaw-dropping awesomeness, the sunsets of the summer monsoon—when skies are crowded with looming thunderclouds, curtains of rain, and leaping electricity— are unsurpassed. Other than the danger of being struck by lightning, there's simply no excuse for staying indoors on an August evening!

Related questions:

Q1. What exactly is a desert?
Q2. Why is the Sonoran Desert so hot and dry?
Q3. Are there seasons in the Sonoran Desert?
Q30. What might I bring on a hike to help me enjoy the desert? (sidebar, page 92)

VOLCANIC SUNSETS

The clarity of desert skies gives Sonoran Desert dwellers good seats for a celestial spectacular usually repeated only a few times in a lifetime, when a powerful volcanic eruption somewhere in the world blasts gas and dust into the **stratosphere**. The dust and tiny droplets of sulfuric acid, created by the reaction of volcanic gases with water vapor, are quickly spread around the globe by high-altitude winds.

The stratospheric haze creates a stunning sunset afterglow, sometimes fading from purple to blood-red, stretching out the twilight long after the sun has set. The most celebrated such performances happened after the island of Krakatau blew itself off the map of Southeast Asia in 1883. Much more recently, the 1991 eruption of Mt. Pinatubo in the Philippines brightened twilights worldwide for many months—a vivid reminder of the finite size of planet Earth.

QUESTION
◆5◆

How can I tell cacti from other spiny desert plants?

ANSWER: *The surest way is by their flowers.*

Colloquially, almost any spiny, thorny, or prickly desert plant is likely to be called a "cactus," but scientifically speaking only members of the botanical family Cactaceae truly deserve the name. Botanists group related plants into families largely by the structures of their reproductive parts; for flowering plants this means the design of their flowers.

This habit of botanists works well because of a peculiarity of plant evolution. When many species of plants evolve from a common ancestor their above-ground growing parts—stems and leaves—often diverge widely in appearance, but their reproductive parts tend to remain remarkably similar. You might never guess that a strawberry plant is related to a pear tree, but their flowers tell us they're cousins. (Both belong to the rose family.)

Fortunately, flowers in the cactus family are easy to recognize. (See diagram.) Here are some of their more distinctive characteristics.

1. Many sepals and petals, grading into each other. In many other kinds of flowers there are a few green sepals that cover the closed bud then open to reveal a few colorful petals. In cacti there are many of both, and you can't always tell which is which.

2. Numerous stamens. Stamens are the male, pollen-bearing parts of a flower. Cactus flowers have too many to easily count— usually hundreds— crowded together inside the cup formed by the petals and sepals.

3. Several stigmas. Stigmas are the sticky flower parts that receive pollen during pollination. In cactus flowers there are three to twenty stigmas, often forming a miniature starburst at the

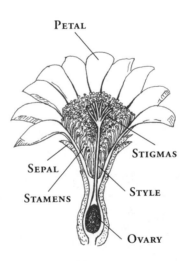

PETAL

STIGMAS

SEPAL

STYLE

STAMENS

OVARY

Saguaro flower

PRICKLY CHARACTERS

In learning to recognize cacti, it helps to become familiar with some of the many forms they take. Here are the major groups in the United States. (A few of our cacti don't fit into these categories, and bear in mind that injury and disease can give rise to some very odd cactus shapes. No one said this would be easy.)

1. HEDGEHOGS
Small plants (usually under two feet tall), often with multiple stems, looking much like miniature columnar cacti.

2. BARRELS
Ridged, usually medium-size globular or barrel-shaped plants, but sometimes more cylindrical and up to eight feet tall.

3. PRICKLY PEARS
Stems composed of many flat segments (pads).

4. CHOLLAS
Stems composed of many lumpy cylindrical segments.

5. PINCUSHIONS
Very small (usually less than four inches tall), with many small bumps instead of ridges, and often densely cloaked with spines.

6. COLUMNAR CACTI
Tall, ridged, cylindrical stems, sometimes clustered or branched.

1.   2.   3.   4.   5.   6.

top of an elongated structure (a style) that rises through the forest of stamens.

4. *Inferior ovary.* This has nothing to do with the quality of the flower's female parts! It's just a botanist's way of saying that the part of the flower that eventually turns into the fruit is sunk below the petals and sepals rather than sitting above them, as in many other flowers.

◆ *What if the plant doesn't have any flowers?*

Don't despair! Even when a cactus has no flowers—the situation most of the year—you usually can tell it's a cactus. Even botanists frequently recognize cacti by characteristics other than their flowers (though they're sometimes loath to admit it). There are several things to look for, at least in plants native to the United States.

1. *Succulent stems.* Actually, this most obvious cactus trait may be the least useful for identification. Succulence may not be very apparent in some cacti (like pencil chollas) and some non-cacti have succulent stems, too.

2. *No leaves.* Don't be confused by prickly pears. Their pads aren't leaves but stem segments, flattened versions of the cylindrical joints of chollas. (But both prickly pears and chollas *do* have tiny vestigial leaves on their young growth. These don't

last long, and they're easy to miss, but they make chollas and prickly pears true exceptions to the no-leaves rule.)

3. *Spines grouped at areoles.* This is actually one of the best ways to recognize a cactus. An **areole** is a specialized organ on the surface of a cactus—a small cushion-like structure from which the spines grow. Often each areole bears spines of several sizes and shapes in a neat geometrical arrangement. If the cactus is lumpy, like chollas and pincushions, there will be an areole on each lump. If the cactus is ridged, like saguaros and barrels, the areoles will be lined up on the ridges.

If you're outside the United States, beware! These rules may not all apply. Elsewhere in the New World you may find cacti with only a single spine at each areole, or with ordinary leaves. And if you're looking at a plant in a garden, all bets are off. It may be a cactus look-alike imported from the Old World. (See Question 6 sidebar, page 22.)

Related questions:

Q6. Which Sonoran Desert plants are most often mistaken for cacti?
Q14. How should I transplant cacti? (sidebar, page 46)
Q32. If I run out of water in the desert can I get some from a barrel cactus?
Q33. Are cactus spines poisonous?

QUESTION
◆ 6

Which Sonoran Desert plants are most often mistaken for cacti?

ANSWER: *There are many, but most are members of the agave family.*

Here are the most notorious charlatans in Arizona and California. Almost all grow not only in desert habitats, but also in nearby semiarid grasslands and woodlands—some are actually much more common in such places.

All but one of these impostors belong to the agave family (Agavaceae), an interesting group related to the lily and the amaryllis. (Some botanists say they actually *are* members of the lily and amaryllis families, or just the lily family. Scientists love to argue.) For the botanically inclined: flowers of agave family members are borne on stalks above clusters of leaves, and usually have three sepals, three petals, and six stamens. They're very different from cactus flowers. And, of course, few cacti have leaves. (See Question 5.)

YUCCAS (*Yucca* species)
Agave family (Agavaceae)
Numerous species, including the Joshua tree *(Yucca brevifolia)* of the Mohave Desert. Stiff, spine-tipped leaves surround the stems, and white flowers (sometimes tinged with green or purple) bloom on a stalk in the spring or early summer.

AGAVES (*Agave* species)
Agave family (Agavaceae)
Many species. Most agaves spend years growing a ground-level cluster of spine-tipped (and usually prickly-edged) leaves, then die when they produce a flower stalk. Flower colors vary, and the leaves may be thick and fleshy, as in the large agaves called "century plants," or stiff and yuccalike, as in the small amole.

SOTOL (*Dasylirion wheeleri*)
Agave family (Agavaceae)
A rounded mass of flexible, straplike leaves edged with curved prickles. In the summer it sends up a stalk densely covered

Yucca

Agave

LOOK-ALIKES

There are many reasons why one kind of living thing may look like another. Usually it's simply because they're related (see Question 10). But sometimes an organism mimics another's appearance, thereby deceiving an unsuspecting third party (Question 38). And sometimes living things come to resemble each other by adapting in similar ways to similar habitats or ways of life—a process called **convergent evolution.**

Cacti and the most cactuslike members of the agave family—agaves, yuccas, and sotol—have evolved similar adaptations to drought. All have more or less succulent tissues that store water, thick skins that keep it from evaporating, and spines or prickles that guard it against thirsty animals. They have less visible similarities, too. Still, agaves, yuccas, and sotol don't really look much like cacti.

The most remarkable cactus look-alikes grow in the Old World. Certain members of the spurge family (Euphorbiaceae) in African and Asian deserts look so much like cacti that even a careless botanist can be fooled. A careful botanist looks to the flowers, though—and finds that those of the succulent euphorbs are much like those of their close relative, the poinsettia. Interestingly, there are euphorbs in the Sonoran Desert also, but they're mostly small ground-hugging plants we barely notice.

Convergent evolution is common among animals, too—but that's another story. (See Question 32 sidebar, page 98.)

with tiny whitish flowers. Often called "desert spoon" because of the spoon-shaped bases of leaves fallen from dead plants.

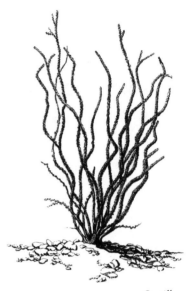

Ocotillo

OCOTILLO
(Fouquieria splendens)
Candlewood family (Fouquieriaceae)

Tall thorny stems bearing red flower clusters at the tips, usually in the spring. Bright green leaves appear soon after soaking rains and are later shed when the soil dries.

Related questions:

Q5. How can I tell cacti from other spiny desert plants?
Q13. Do I need to water native desert plants? (sidebar, page 45)
Q14. How should I transplant cacti? (sidebar, page 46)

QUESTION
7

How old do desert plants get?

ANSWER: *In most cases we can only make an educated guess.*

Botanists have little firm information about the maximum ages of desert plants growing in the wild, but they've combined precious bits of hard data with casual observations, anecdotes, tantalizing clues, and a healthy dose of scientific intuition to come up with some reasonable estimates. The table on page 25 lists those estimates for a few common desert plants. Some of these numbers are much more secure than others.

You'll have to decide for yourself whether or not to think of any of these plants as truly old. Take the saguaro for example. (Its maximum age is better established than most of the others in the table.) Compared to the human lifespan, two hundred years is surely a long time, and it may seem like a surprisingly ripe old age for a cactus. But at two centuries a bristlecone pine would be just getting started—some are more than four thousand years old!

Fishhook barrel cactus

People are naturally curious about the oldest desert plants, but species at the other end of the lifespan spectrum are interesting, too. Many desert **annual** wildflowers sprout, bloom, drop their seeds and die during a single rainy season. Some complete their life cycle within a few weeks, an abbreviated existence that earns them the name **ephemerals.**

One of the marvelous things about the Sonoran Desert is that despite its seemingly harsh climate there can be so many life strategies that work, and a tiny ephemeral wildflower can dash through its life in the shadow of an ancient ironwood tree.

◆ *Why don't we know more about the maximum ages of desert plants?*

The information is hard to come by. Growth rings, an obvious place to look, are difficult to interpret in most desert trees. Some **dendrochronologists** believe these plants respond to sporadic rains by laying down multiple rings in a single growing season. This could make the years impossible to count. But it may be that scientists accustomed to the neat rings of conifers just haven't yet learned to read the more obscure records written in the wood of paloverdes and mesquites.

Radiocarbon dating has yielded some information. Tiny amounts of carbon-14, a rare radioactive form (isotope) of carbon, are incorporated into the tissues of living things along with ordinary carbon-12. After death the carbon-14 is gradually depleted by radioactive decay; measuring how much is left gives an estimate of age. But for technical reasons it's difficult to use this method for materials less than about three hundred years old—and few desert species seem to live longer than that.

Rephotography is starting to provide some answers. If the same plant shows up in two photographs of a scene taken fifty

QUEEN CLONE?

Can a creosote bush really live twelve thousand years? It depends on how you look at it.

A creosote bush doesn't have a single trunk; it has multiple branches arising from a "stem crown" near ground level. As the crown grows its center dies, leaving a ring of living tissue. Over many years the ring increases in diameter, then eventually breaks up into an expanding circle of separate plants. All these plants are genetically identical descendants of the original bush: a **clone**.

One very large creosote bush clone in the Mohave Desert—the famous "King Clone," sometimes called the world's oldest plant—has been estimated to have started from a single seedling nearly twelve thousand years ago. (Many botanists suggest a somewhat lesser age.) But the living stems and roots of each separate bush are less than two hundred years old.

Clones challenge our common-sense notion of what we mean by an individual animal or plant. Some biologists like to think of a clone as a single living thing with many disconnected parts, but this is a very strange idea for most of us. Jumping and teddy bear chollas regularly clone themselves from detached joints, yet no one thinks of calling a cholla patch the oldest plant in the world!

Even some "species" of desert lizards are actually clones. Sonoran spotted whiptails are all **parthenogenetic** females: they have offspring without the help of males. How long ago was the original for all of today's copies? Would you consider this entire reptilian sisterhood, collectively, a candidate for the desert's oldest lizard?

Sonoran spotted whiptail

ESTIMATED MAXIMUM AGES OF
SOME SONORAN DESERT PLANTS

30+ years
ENGELMANN PRICKLY PEAR
(*Opuntia phaeacantha* var. *discata*)

40 years
GOLDEN AGAVE
(*Agave chrysantha*)

50 years
TRIANGLE-LEAF BURSAGE
(*Ambrosia deltoidea*)

60+ years
TEDDY BEAR CHOLLA
(*Opuntia bigelovii*)

130+ years
FISHHOOK BARREL CACTUS
(*Ferocactus wislizeni*)

130+ years
CATCLAW ACACIA
(*Acacia greggii*)

200 years
OCOTILLO
(*Fouquieria splendens*)

200+ years
SAGUARO
(*Carnegiea gigantea*)

200+ years
FOOTHILL PALOVERDE
(*Cercidium microphyllum*)

800+ years
IRONWOOD
(*Olneya tesota*)

12,000? years
CREOSOTE BUSH
(*Larrea tridentata*)

years apart, you know the species can live at least that long. Few useful photographs of the Sonoran Desert go back much more than a century, but as time passes they'll become more and more revealing. (The moral? Hang onto your snapshots. A few centuries from now someone may be more interested in the shrub in the background than in Aunt Jane's smile!)

Related questions:

Q5. How can I tell cacti from other spiny desert plants?
Q6. Which Sonoran Desert plants are most often mistaken for cacti?
Q8. Are saguaros endangered?
Q13. Do I need to water native desert plants? (sidebar, page 45)

Phainopepla on a mesquite branch

QUESTION

◆ 8 ◆

Are saguaros endangered?

ANSWER: *No, saguaros aren't threatened by extinction.*

But, there have been enough "vanishing saguaro" scares over the years to give many people the wrong idea.

Scare number one. About 1940 a plant pathologist reported that many saguaros in Arizona, including a fifth of those in the famous Cactus Forest of Saguaro National Monument, east of Tucson (now part of Saguaro National Park), showed obvious signs of decay. A bacterium in the blackened and oozing tissues was soon identified as the pathogen of a deadly "bacterial necrosis disease." Rotting saguaros in the Monument were cut down in a "disease control" experiment, living cacti were injected with penicillin, and it was even proposed that the entire Cactus Forest be sprayed with DDT to kill insects suspected of spreading the affliction!

False alarm. Bacterial necrosis is now thought to be just the natural decay of cactus tissues killed or weakened by something else, and few scientists still call it a disease. Saguaros, especially the very old and very young, are sensitive to subfreezing temperatures, and the "outbreak" in the Cactus Forest probably stemmed from a severe frost a few years earlier. Nevertheless, the myth of an insidious cactus plague lives stubbornly on.

Scare number two. As many spectacular older saguaros in the Cactus Forest succumbed to freezing and other natural causes, it became painfully evident that there were few young cacti to grow up and take their place. Concern grew about a possible breakdown in saguaro reproduction, and after the 1960s it focused on the apparent decline in southern Arizona of a saguaro pollinator, the lesser

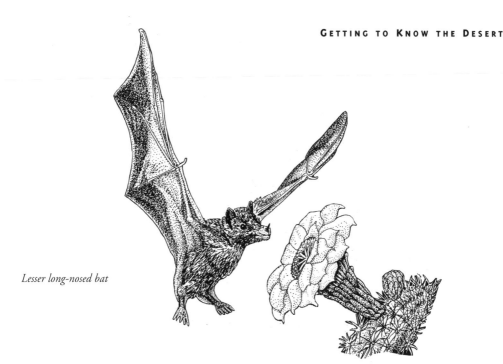

Lesser long-nosed bat

long-nosed bat (*Leptonycteris curasoae*). Partly as a result of fears for the future of the saguaro, the bat was listed as endangered in 1988.

False alarm. Saguaro flowers unfold long after dark and stay open until the next afternoon. Nectar-feeding bats do pollinate them at night, but after sunrise they're visited by a host of other pollinators, including birds, native insects, and honey bees (an Old World introduction—see Question 23). Bats are wonderful creatures, but saguaros would presumably go on making more saguaros without them.

Other factors probably accounted for the missing juveniles in the Cactus Forest (see below). Young cacti have made a comeback there in recent decades.

Scare number three. In the early 1990s researchers called attention to a degeneration of the skin (epidermis) of some saguaros at Saguaro National Monument. Air pollution from nearby Tucson was first proposed as a cause of this "epidermal browning," then sunburning by **ultraviolet** rays—the hypothetical consequence of a world-wide thinning of the **ozone layer.** The phenomenon was quickly connected with the by then well-publicized decline of the Cactus Forest, once again raising the specter of the saguaro's imminent demise.

False alarm. The jury is still out on the causes of epidermal browning—it may just be the result of heat, drought, and old age—but there's no evidence that it by itself causes death or reproductive failure. Like bacterial necrosis, epidermal browning is a widespread natural process, and nothing new. It may make some saguaros less photogenic, but it won't make them all disappear.

◆ *Aren't there any real threats to saguaros?*

There certainly are. Aside from freezing weather, lightning, high winds,

WHY SO MANY FALSE ALARMS ABOUT SAGUAROS?

People love saguaros. They're conspicuous and beautiful plants, they symbolize the American Southwest, and their trunk and arms lend them a human quality. When we perceive a threat to the saguaro it can seem like an old friend is in trouble. Unfortunately, our natural concerns have sometimes led scientists, the newsmedia, and the public astray.

We're also easily misled by the perspective of our limited lifespan. We experience change on a scale of decades, but a population of saguaros may fluctuate in size and age makeup on a scale of centuries. This is a natural consequence of a fickle desert climate. Numerous saguaro seedlings may sprout during an especially wet monsoon, mature many decades later into an unusually populous stand, then almost all be killed by a single frost. Such die-backs may happen over and over again, but when we see only one in our lifetime it can seem like an unprecedented disaster.

On the positive side, our affection for saguaros has made them among the most-studied wild plants on earth. We can be sure that if this species ever becomes truly endangered, someone will notice!

and hungry desert creatures, individual saguaros fall victim to cactus rustlers and vandals. They're drowned by reservoirs, and destroyed or relocated—often unsuccessfully—for construction projects. In some places, cattle grazing and wood-cutting have removed the **nurse plants** that young saguaros need for survival (probably the main cause of the temporary lack of baby saguaros in the Cactus Forest). But none of these factors threatens the species overall.

Another problem has recently caught the attention of biologists. Wildfire was once relatively rare in Sonoran Desert ecosystems, but in some areas Old World grasses have invaded the spaces between the native plants and provided fuel to carry the flames. Most native desert plants—saguaros included—are easily killed by fire. What's more, loss of the natives may make the desert more hospitable to the invaders, starting a vicious cycle that could result in permanent changes in some areas.

False alarm? No, the problem is real—but it won't threaten the saguaro with extinction. The Sonoran Desert our great grandchildren will see may differ from ours in many ways, but there should still be saguaros for them to enjoy—and probably worry about!

Related questions:

Q1. What exactly is a desert?
Q3. Are there seasons in the Sonoran Desert?
Q7. How old do desert plants get?
Q23. How can I tell if the bees in my yard are Africanized?

QUESTION

◆
9

What are the frogs I hear at night during the summer rains?

ANSWER: *They may be spadefoot toads.*

If they are, you have a chance to meet one of the Sonoran Desert's most remarkable creatures! Spadefoot toads, or just "spadefoots" for short, are toadlike amphibians, but technically not really toads. True toads are members of the zoological family Bufonidae, but spadefoots belong to the family Pelobatidae.

Actually, it's possible you're hearing true toads, not spadefoots. Further investigation is in order.

◆ How can I tell whether they're spadefoots or true toads?

The very first night you hear them calling, grab a flashlight and head for the sound. It will probably lead you to a temporary rain pond. There will be more out there than you and the amphibians, so watch for rattlesnakes! (See Question 37.)

Now the real fun begins. You have to catch one. If you had a deprived childhood and never learned frog-catching skills, this may take a while. Hint: sometimes it helps to shine your flashlight in their faces.

Once you have the squirming, slippery creature firmly (but gently) in hand, look at its eyes. True toads have horizontal pupils, but spadefoots have vertical pupils (like cats). Then look behind the eyes. Toads have a raised poison gland behind each eye; spadefoots don't.

◆ How can I tell the species?

If you've got a true toad, consult one of the field guides listed in the bibliography. There are several species in the Sonoran Desert. (If your hunt led you to a stream

Couch's spadefoot

or a perennial pond, there are still other possibilities besides toads and spadefoots. Good reading!)

If you're sure it's a spadefoot, look at the sole of a hind foot. There you'll find the hard, dark "spade" that gives a spadefoot its name. There are only two spadefoot

Couch's
spadefoot

Western
spadefoot

(Redrawn from Stebbins, *A Field Guide to Western Reptiles and Amphibians.*)

species in the Sonoran Desert of Arizona and California. If the spade is sickle-shaped, it's Couch's spadefoot, *Scaphiopus couchi*. If the spade is rounded, it's the western spadefoot, *Scaphiopus hammondii* (called the southern spadefoot, *Scaphiopus multiplicatus*, in some field guides).

The skin secretions of western spadefoots smell like roasted peanuts and may make you sneeze. They're also especially toxic, so be extra sure to wash your hands after handling one of these creatures.

Incidentally, the spades really are digging tools—spadefoots use them to burrow backward into the soil.

Once you've finished checking the animal, gently put it down where you caught it—it has important things to do—then wash your hands thoroughly in the water. Amphibian skin secretions can be quite toxic; they probably won't affect your hands, but you won't want to get them in your eyes, nose, or mouth. (See Question 35.)

◆ Why are spadefoots so noisy?

Spadefoots live for the **monsoon.** They spend the rest of the year underground awaiting their wake-up call: the drumming of raindrops on the soil during a summer thunderstorm. As soon as the males dig out they go looking for rain pools, and when they find them they broadcast the news as loudly as they can. The chorus draws silent female spadefoots (and naturalists of both sexes) from far and wide.

Sometimes several kinds of hopping amphibians converge on the same pond. Their different calls help the females find males of the right species (see sidebar, next page), but the males grasp anything toad-like they encounter in the dark. It's an orgy rivalling anything in ancient Rome. You may want to stay and watch.

Mating is an urgent matter for spadefoots. Their tadpoles must hatch, grow, and change into toadlets before the pool evaporates in the summer sun. That's why they do most of their mating the first night the pool forms (and why you shouldn't wait until tomorrow if you want to see it). Couch's spadefoot toadlets sometimes leave the puddle only nine days after the eggs are laid! Western spadefoots take longer—at least three weeks.

• How do spadefoot tadpoles grow up so fast?

Summer rainstorms wash leaves, rabbit droppings, and other organic debris into the ponds. The sun cooks it all into a nutritious soup, teeming with algae and bacteria. Sometimes small crustaceans like fairy shrimp, which laid eggs before the ponds dried up in previous years, hatch out and feed on the microorganisms.

NIGHT MUSIC

Spadefoot species rely on their distinctive calls to sort themselves out in the dark and you, too, may find them useful for identification. Here are some of the ways they've been described. What do they sound like to you?

COUCH'S SPADEFOOT
"A person moaning"
"The bleating of an anxious sheep"

WESTERN SPADEFOOT
"The purring of a cat, but stronger"
"A hoarse snore"
"A person sawing wood"
"A thumbnail dragged across the teeth of a comb"

The warmth of the water speeds up the tadpoles' growth. Meanwhile they devour everything even remotely edible. They scrape algae off rocks. They filter microorganisms from the water as they pump it over their gills. They gather in wriggling masses, stir up the muck on the bottom of the pond, and filter that. And unlike most tadpoles, which are exclusively **herbivores** and filter-feeders, spadefoot tadpoles are **omnivores.** They also eat dead insects and tadpoles, and they prey on live fairy shrimp.

Fairy shrimp

Western spadefoots go a step further. If the puddle is crowded and prey is abundant, a few of the tadpoles change into oversized, voracious **carnivores.** These even go after other tadpoles. They prefer different species, but they'll eat their own kind, too—bad news for their relatives, but it gives the cannibals a critical advantage in the life and death race against evaporation.

Related questions:

Q3. Are there seasons in the Sonoran Desert?
Q34. Why don't I see very many animals when I hike in the desert? (sidebar, page 104)
Q35. How dangerous are Sonoran Desert toads?
Q37. How can I avoid dangerous encounters with rattlers and Gila monsters?

Is a javelina a pig?

ANSWER: *No, javelina and pigs are members of different zoological families.*

The javelina, or collared peccary, is one of three members of the peccary family (Tayassuidae). True pigs, including about nine wild species, belong to the Old World swine family (Suidae). The familiar barnyard pig is a domesticated form of one member of the Old World swine family, the wild boar.

To be fair, though, many people—including some scientists—use the word "pig" for members of both families.

The Desert Museum prefers to reserve that word for the Old World swine, which differ from peccaries in many interesting ways, as we shall see.

• *If javelina aren't pigs, then why do they look like pigs?*

Javelina resemble pigs for essentially the same reason people resemble their cousins: they have common ancestors.

However, the last common ancestors of pigs and peccaries lived tens of millions of years ago, early in the Age of Mammals (Cenozoic Era). By about thirty million years ago pigs and peccaries were already trotting down separate evolutionary paths.

How closely are pigs and peccaries related? To put it in perspective, the human family (Hominidae) and the ape family (Pongidae) had common ancestors much more recently—well within the last ten million years. By that standard, pigs and peccaries are considerably more distantly related than people and chimpanzees!

• How are javelina different from pigs?

Some of the more interesting differences are these:

Size. Javelina are much smaller than pigs. Adult javelina weigh roughly fifty pounds, while some species of wild pigs weigh a dozen times that much.

Anatomy. The large **canine teeth** ("tusks") of javelina are straight, while the canines of pigs curve outward, as in wart-hogs (an African species of wild pig). All peccaries have a scent gland on the rear of the back, something completely lacking in pigs. (See sidebar, this page.)

Feeding. Javelina are almost entirely **herbivorous,** though they do occasionally eat insects and carrion. Pigs are much more **omnivorous;** some even eat small rodents and birds.

Social behavior. Javelina are highly social. They form permanent herds with frequent

PECCARY PERFUME

Usually hidden beneath the bristly hairs near the rear of a javelina's back is a small organ producing an oily liquid with a strong and unmistakable odor. This musky perfume helps maintain order in the busy javelina social life.

Javelina usually stay with the same herds throughout their lives, traveling, feeding, bedding down, even playing together. From time to time pairs of animals stand nose-to-tail and rub their heads across each other's scent glands. As a result of this frequent contact, every javelina herd develops its own distinctive group scent.

Javelina sniff each other to recognize their herd-mates. As the herd moves through the desert it's enveloped by its communal smell, helping members to stay in contact with the group. (They also listen for the sounds of the other animals' grunting, chewing, and moving about.)

Odor also helps keep different herds apart. Herds mark the boundaries of their territories by rubbing scent glands across rocks and trees.

intimate contact, much cooperation, and little competition between members. Wild pigs tend to form more temporary groups, and the males, especially, are much more competitive.

Reproduction. Javelina typically bear two young per litter, while wild pigs often have twice that many or more. Baby javelina are able to walk along with the herd only hours after birth (they're **precocial**). Newborn piglets are nearly helpless and must stay with the sow in a nest or den (they're **altricial**).

Geography. Peccaries all live in the New World tropics and subtropics, while pigs would be entirely an Old World group if they hadn't been imported to the Americas by Europeans. (All New World wild pigs, including the ill-tempered "razorbacks" of the southeastern United States, descend from escaped domestic swine or wild boar released for sport hunting.)

◆ *Are javelina really nearly blind?*

Javelina have difficulty seeing distant objects. They probably can't perceive a moving person more than seventy-five yards away, and when they're busy feeding they'll sometimes approach within a few feet of a person who's standing still (and downwind).

Javelina use their vision mostly for feeding and up-close interactions with each other, and depend mostly on their senses of hearing and smell for longer-range information gathering. By human standards they're nearsighted, but by javelina standards their eyes are just right—and our noses are woefully inadequate.

◆ *Are javelina dangerous?*

Not unless you create a dangerous situation. If a herd of javelina detects you at a distance (usually by odor), they will beat an orderly retreat. However, if you sneak up and startle the animals they're liable to bolt suddenly in random directions. It's unlikely any will actually attack, but when a nearsighted creature with sharp tusks is bearing down on you at high velocity the distinction seems unimportant!

Another way to create a dangerous situation is to feed javelina. As with almost any wild mammal, repeated feeding breaks down their natural fear of humans. Once the javelina cease keeping their distance the chances of an unfortunate encounter greatly increase. Hand feeding is especially dangerous—you may get bitten.

Related questions:

Q16. How can I keep wild animals from eating the plants in my garden?
Q17. How can I attract desert wildlife to my yard?

QUESTION

11

How do Sonoran Desert cities get their water?

ANSWER: *It isn't easy.*

Like cities anywhere, Sonoran Desert cities tap into groundwater, surface water, or a combination of the two. But, as you might expect, in a desert both kinds of water are much more difficult to acquire.

♦ What are the sources of surface water for desert cities?

Since rainfall is so sparse in the Sonoran Desert, the sources of its rivers (and the lakes we create by damming them) lie elsewhere—often well outside the desert. For example, the Phoenix area receives much of its water from dams on the Salt and Verde Rivers, which flow from wetter mountainous regions north and east of the city. Communities along the Colorado River benefit from rain and snow that falls as far away as Utah and Colorado. And Central Arizona Project canals now carry Colorado River water hundreds of miles outside the river basin to Phoenix and Tucson.

Taking water from desert rivers for cities, mines, and farms has consequences for these watercourses. Today barely a trickle usually reaches the Gulf of California via the broad channel of the Colorado. Other important desert rivers have been reduced to dry **washes** and **arroyos** (see sidebar, next page). As a result, many native desert fishes are now threatened and endangered, and much of the original **riparian** habitat so valuable to desert wildlife has been diminished or lost.

♦ What are the sources of groundwater for desert cities?

Large amounts of water lie beneath the surface in the valleys between Sonoran Desert mountain ranges, and desert communities have sunk wells to reach them. These **aquifers** aren't subterranean lakes, though. A simple thought experiment may help to visualize them.

Imagine filling a glass jar to the rim with sand, then adding water until the water line is an inch below the top. The sand represents the sediments under a desert valley, and the wet portion, where water fills the spaces between the grains, is the aquifer. The water line, of course, is the **water table** which must be reached by a city's wells.

Where does the water in the aquifers come from? Some comes from outside the desert: it percolates through the beds of rivers that originate in wetter regions.

RIVERS OF SAND

Dry rivers are a puzzle for newcomers to the Sonoran Desert. How can they be called "rivers" at all, and why do some have cities on their banks? Answer: they were "real" rivers once.

Phoenix is where it is because in the 1860s the Salt River and its tributary, the Verde, flowed dependably enough to irrigate farms. In fact, the city rose (something like the mythical being for which it was named) on the ruins of an earlier agricultural civilization. The prehistoric Hohokam Indians had built extensive canals there centuries before. Today, except for occasional floods and areas watered by treated sewage effluent, the Salt is bone dry. All its water is diverted by dams upstream.

The Santa Cruz River at Tucson is in similar condition, though it has no major dams. Irrigation practices and erosion caused by overgrazing probably contributed to a sudden down-cutting of the riverbed in the late 1800s. (The phenomenon still isn't completely understood.) A dropping water table later dried out what was left of the river. Looking at this river of sand today, it's hard to imagine that when the Tucson presidio was founded in 1776 parts of the Santa Cruz flowed year-round between lushly vegetated banks, and the Spanish garrison could watch O'odham Indians tending farms on the floodplain!

Additional water derives from local rain and snow, including what falls in desert mountain ranges. But much of the water in desert aquifers is very ancient. It filtered into the ground during a much rainier time—the **Pleistocene period,** which ended about eleven thousand years ago. It's truly "fossil water."

◆ Is there enough water?

Sonoran Desert aquifers are like water bank accounts. We inherited a healthy balance, but now every year withdrawals exceed deposits. Water tables in some places are dropping several feet per year. Eventually the accounts will be depleted unless we change our spending habits.

Meanwhile, descending water tables dry out desert streams and their **riparian** vegetation. And as the water is removed from between the grains of underground sediments the surface of the land sinks. When such **subsidence** is uneven it can cause cracks in soil, roads, pipes, and buildings. Bringing water from distant rivers reduces our groundwater dependency, and some of the imported water may even be used for recharging aquifers. But there are already too many demands on many of these desert rivers.

Sonoran Desert cities won't become dry ghost towns anytime soon, but it's clear we need to make significant changes if millions of us are to continue to live where water is scarce. Some adjustments will involve agriculture and industry, but there are also many things we can do as individuals—beginning with conserving water in our own homes. We still have much to learn about living where it's dry, and getting to know the experts—the desert's own cacti and kangaroo rats—is a great way to start.

Related questions:

Q1. What exactly is a desert?
Q2. Why is the Sonoran Desert so hot and dry?
Q12. How did Indians live in the Sonoran Desert?
Q13. Do I need to water native desert plants?

Grasshopper mouse

How did Indians live
in the Sonoran Desert?

ANSWER: *They depended on an intimate knowledge of the desert world of which they were a part.*

Three hundred years ago a number of related groups, speaking dialects of a common language, lived in a large area of what is now southwestern Arizona and northwestern Sonora. The Spaniards gave these desert dwellers many names (Pima, Papago, Sobaipuri, and others), but the Indians called themselves *O'odham*, or "the People." Other native people lived elsewhere in the Sonoran Desert, but the O'odham illustrate well how human beings met the challenges—and opportunities—of life in this arid land.

The O'odham homeland wasn't a uniform environment. It encompassed a spectrum of climates, from the very dry Lower Colorado River Valley on the west to the Arizona Upland on the east, with its much greater summer rainfall (see Question 2). Perennial rivers, which arose outside the desert, marked its borders but not its interior. Across this varied landscape, the O'odham way of life varied as well.

RIVER PEOPLE

Along the rivers (except the Colorado and the Lower Gila, which were occupied by other Indians) the River People lived in permanent villages and planted corn, beans, squash, and cotton on floodplains moistened and fertilized by summer overflow. (Such agriculture would be impossible on most of these rivers today—see Question 11.) The rivers, as well as the natural **riparian** vegetation and wildlife they supported, provided an abundance of wild resources, but the River People still made frequent forays into the desert to hunt and gather, as did their relatives living in more arid areas.

TWO-VILLAGE PEOPLE

In the Arizona Upland, but away from the rivers, lived the Two-Village People. During the winter they occupied villages near perennial springs in the mountain foothills, but with the coming of the summer rains they moved down to other villages in the valleys. There they relied for drinking water on runoff collected in natural and artificial basins (charcos), and

They subsisted mostly on wild foods, which were diverse and often abundant in the relatively moist Arizona Upland. While some desert plant foods, like sweet saguaro fruits, were obvious and immediately appetizing, others, like roots and tubers, were hidden, or like spiny cholla buds, required special preparation. The O'odham knew not only which plants were useful and how to prepare them, but

---

WHERE ARE THE O'ODHAM TODAY?

By far the majority of modern O'odham live in the United States, roughly half of them on six reservations in their ancestral homelands. They are members of two official tribes, the Pima and the Tohono O'odham (Desert People; formerly the Papago).

As with most Native Americans, European goods, customs, and technologies have greatly altered their ways of life, and many of the changes have been stressful. A calorie-rich diet has led to widespread diabetes; alcoholism and unemployment are frequent problems.

As the O'odham seek their cultural balance, efforts are being made by some to preserve important traditions amidst the pervasive influences of American culture. Finding a sustainable way of life in the Sonoran Desert for the twenty-first century will be a challenge for them—as it will be for us all.

---

they planted crops similar to those of the River People in ground dampened by flash floods at the mouths of desert washes.

This desert-adapted agriculture, called *ak chin* (arroyo mouth) or de temporal (rainy weather) cultivation, was always chancy, depending on the desert's unpredictable rainfall. It worked because centuries of trial and error had led to the evolution not only of exquisitely adapted crop plants, but of a whole interdependent collection of pollinators, edible "weeds," and even edible pests (like rabbits)—a rich ecosystem of which the skilled farmers were themselves a part.

Still, farming provided only a part of the nutrition of the Two-Village People.

also exactly where and when to find each one. This knowledge, and the skills necessary to hunt desert game, were a cultural treasure every bit as valuable as the plants and animals themselves.

SAND PEOPLE

Farther west, in the very arid Lower Colorado River Valley (but not along the river itself), the O'odham lived mostly without agriculture or permanent houses and adopted a purely nomadic existence, following resources as they became available seasonally or in response to unpredictable desert rains. Their subsistence in this severe environment is a tribute to human ingenuity.

The nomadic Sand People found water at a small number of springs and natural stone tanks (**tinajas**) in the low mountain ranges, and carried it through the desert in hollowed-out gourds. Like other O'odham, they hunted not only large game—mountain sheep, pronghorn, and deer—but also rabbits, packrats, quail, lizards, and insects. From time to time they visited the Gulf of California to fish and gather shellfish.

Like their relatives to the east, the Sand People collected plant foods such as cactus fruits, agave hearts, beans of desert trees, and wild greens, but these resources were less abundant than in the Arizona Upland. Less rainfall meant fewer plants, fewer animals, and fewer people. There were probably never more than a few hundred of these resourceful nomads—fewer than the number of students in typical elementary school in modern-day Tucson or Phoenix—spread through an area of thousands of square miles.

The Sand People seemed materially poor to the Spaniards who encountered them in late seventeenth century, but they usually had enough to meet their needs. Nor were they impoverished in other ways. Like all O'odham, they spoke a complex language, slept under the stars in a beautiful landscape, and led lives of cooperation and generosity, ceremony and prayer. When the Sand People traded for pottery and agricultural products with their Cocopa neighbors in the Colorado River delta, they offered in return salt, seashells—and ceremonial songs.

Related questions:

Q1. What exactly is a desert?
Q2. Why is the Sonoran Desert so hot and dry?
Q3. Are there seasons in the Sonoran Desert?
Q11. How do Sonoran Desert cities get their water?

Around the Home

THERE'S NO DENYING that living in the desert has its challenges, but they're mostly just variations on situations encountered anywhere. While a desert resident is cursing the rock-hard soil in her garden, someone in the Southeast is bemoaning his soggy clay. The packrat in the garage is just the desert version of the squirrel in the attic, and woodpeckers display no regional prejudice —they torment homeowners everywhere!

The secret to making a home in the desert is to adjust yourself to it, rather than try to adjust it to you. You can save both aggravation and water by growing appropriate plants in your garden, and you can coexist peacefully even with scorpions—if you do your best to keep them outdoors! The next few questions will help you fill in the details.

QUESTION

Do I need to water native desert plants?

ANSWER: *After native desert shrubs, trees, and succulents have become established in a landscape, they ordinarily don't need watering.*

But there are certain situations in which you may want to irrigate:

• When desert landscapes are planted more densely than natural desert plant communities—and they very often are —rainfall may not be enough to support them. You'll probably need to do some supplementary watering.

• While desert plants are experts at surviving droughts, you may not like how they look while they're doing it. You can improve their appearance during a dry period by giving them some water. (But beware: this can take a huge amount of water during the summer heat!)

• Once in a while there's a drought so severe that even some naturally growing desert plants succumb. At such times you may want to ensure the survival of important landscape plants by giving them a drink.

• Some plants that grow naturally in areas of

the Sonoran Desert where there are frequent monsoon thunderstorms may need summer irrigation if you put them in parts of the Lower Colorado River Valley little visited by the monsoon. (See Question 2.)

If an artificial desert landscape were an exact copy of the area's natural plant

community, you'd never have to water it. The need for irrigation arises when we ask more from an arid land than it's ordinarily able to provide.

• Is it possible to over-water native desert plants?

Yes, and people often do it. Don't allow the soil to remain wet for long periods of time. Waterlogging reduces oxygen availability—it literally drowns the roots. Instead, let the soil dry out between waterings. Even bone-dry soil won't kill a well-established desert plant (though it may drop its leaves).

There's even less need to water during the winter, when many Sonoran Desert plants are dormant, though you probably should irrigate winter growers (such as brittlebush) if the weather is very dry. Check with your local nursery or a good landscape book if you're unsure about the growing seasons of any of your desert plants.

If you're careful, it is possible to give your desert landscape a lusher look and

increase the growth rates of your plants by giving them limited extra water. But there can be some unfortunate side-effects— and not just on your water bill! The extra greenery is likely to be weaker, juicier, and lower in chemical defenses against pests, and it may tempt plant-eating wildlife from the surrounding desert.

Plants from other deserts may have different requirements than Sonoran Desert natives. Be sure to find out their growing seasons, water needs, and temperature tolerances.

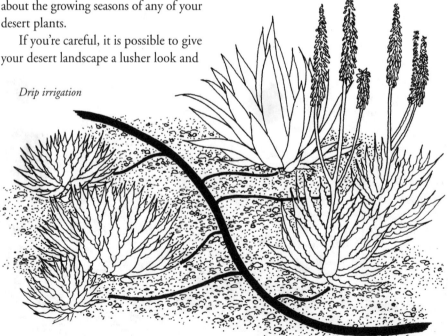

Drip irrigation

LIFE ON THE DRY SIDE

In a desert drought isn't an occasional unfortunate event, it's the natural condition during much of the year. Sonoran Desert plants have evolved many strategies to deal with the inevitable. Here are a few of them.

Succulents harvest rainwater quickly with their wide-spreading, shallow roots, then hoard it in their tissues. Many, including cacti, minimize water loss by opening their pores only in the cool of the night to absorb carbon dioxide for **photosynthesis** the following day—a process called **crassulacean acid metabolism** (CAM). Because of these adaptations, succulents can continue to grow through a typical dry season.

Other desert plants greatly reduce their activities during dry times. **Drought deciduous** plants such as ocotillos and paloverdes drop their leaves, but continue to carry on some photosynthesis in green tissues in their stems. Creosote bushes usually keep their leaves, but seal in their moisture with a resinous **cuticle**. Some **perennial** wildflowers die back to underground roots or bulbs when the soil dries.

Annuals escape droughts entirely. They complete their entire life cycle, from germination through flowering and seed production, all within a single wet season, then pass the droughts as seeds. In the Sonoran Desert there are two main groups of annual wildflowers, winter annuals and summer annuals, adapted to the two periods of rainfall.

If some of this seems to violate common sense, remember that desert plants have evolved not only to tolerate drought, but to require it. It's all too easy to kill them with kindness.

◆ What about winter annual wildflowers?

Native winter annuals are another exception to the rule about winter watering. Sow the seeds when the weather cools in the fall and rake the soil lightly over them. Keep the soil constantly moist until the seeds germinate, then water the seedlings regularly all winter long to make sure the roots never dry out. (You may need to protect the seedlings from hungry animals.) When warm weather arrives in the spring you can help stimulate flowering by temporarily reducing irrigation.

In nature such perfect conditions rarely occur. Only perhaps once a decade on average do the Sonoran Desert's unpredictable rains provide the amount and timing of moisture necessary for a spectacular spring wildflower display—but you can produce one every year!

Related questions:

Q1. What exactly is a desert?
Q2. Why is the Sonoran Desert so hot and dry?
Q3. Are there seasons in the Sonoran Desert?
Q11. How do Sonoran Desert cities get their water?
Q14. How should I transplant cacti?
Q16. How can I keep wild animals from eating the plants in my garden?

QUESTION 14

How should I transplant cacti?

ANSWER: *With a few exceptions, transplanting a cactus isn't much different from transplanting any other plant.*

Cacti are tough. Often it's enough simply to stick one in the ground and leave it alone. But you can increase your plant's chances for surviving the transplanting by taking the following steps:

1. Choose a site where the cactus will receive about the same amount of sunlight as before, then orient the plant so that what was previously the sunniest side still is. That side will be the most resistant to sunburn.

2. Dust wounds on the roots with sulfur to ward off infection.

3. Place the plant no deeper in the ground than it was growing before. The

Prickly pear

DON'T BE A CACTUS RUSTLER!

Cacti, agaves, ocotillos, desert trees, and certain other native Sonoran Desert plants are protected by law in both California and Arizona. Taking these plants (or cuttings) from the wild requires both a permit and the landowner's consent, and a special tag must be attached to each plant before it's transported. For more information, contact the Arizona Department of Agriculture or the California Department of Food and Agriculture. (See the organizations list at the back of this book.)

roots of a cactus need to spread out close to the surface.

4. Back-fill the hole with well-drained soil, not too rocky, then tamp it lightly with a wooden stick to eliminate air pockets without bruising the roots.

5. Wait about two weeks before watering, to give the roots time to heal; then water sparingly during the first growing season (until cold weather).

You can increase your own chances for surviving the transplanting by wearing heavy gloves and being *very* careful.

One of the greatest problems for most transplants is water stress, but that's a condition cacti are superbly adapted to handle. The stored moisture in a cactus buys it time while its roots regrow. Resist the urge to baby it by over-watering and it will probably do fine.

◆ When should I transplant cacti?

Anytime but winter. Despite the common-sense notion that cooler weather should be easier on a transplant, winter is actually the least favorable season for transplanting cacti. A very wet soil caused by heavy winter rains encourages root fungi, and since cacti are mostly dormant during the colder season they have few resources available to fight infection. If you *must* transplant cacti during the winter, don't water them until warm weather arrives.

◆ Do I need to do anything special to transplant saguaros?

Since saguaros are relatively expensive, you'll want to follow all the advice given above, being especially sure to provide water during the first growing season (and

perhaps the second and third). Tempting as it may be to install a mature saguaro in your landscape, few large saguaros survive transplanting. Even professional landscapers have limited success with saguaros more than ten or twelve feet tall, and such big cacti can be dangerous to work with. So choose a young, vigorous plant and cultivate the gardener's most important virtue: patience.

◆ Is it possible to grow cacti from cuttings?

Prickly pears and chollas (genus *Opuntia*) are easy to grow from cuttings. Take a cutting of one or two pads or joints (stem segments), and partially bury it upright in the ground, no more than two inches deep, just enough to give it support. It doesn't require watering. A prickly pear started this way is actually likely to do better than a large transplanted specimen. (Large chollas can often be transplanted more successfully, but they're a real challenge to handle.) Hedgehogs (*Echinocereus*) can be started the same way, but the likelihood of success is much lower. A dusting of sulfur on the wound of any cactus cutting can be helpful.

Related questions:

Q3. Are there seasons in the Sonoran Desert?
Q13. Do I need to water native desert plants?
Q33. Are cactus spines poisonous?

What's the concrete-like stuff buried in my garden?

ANSWER: *It's a natural mineral deposit common in desert soils.*

Soil scientists call it a "calcic horizon" (meaning, essentially, a calcium-rich soil layer), but almost everyone else knows it as **caliche** (kuh-LEE-chee). Caliche is the result of natural processes that deposit lime—calcium carbonate, $CaCO_3$, the stuff of limestone—in arid soils. The lime can take many forms, from chalky powders to veins, lumps, coatings on rocks, and

the thick, cement-hard layers that can be the bane of desert gardeners.

Heavy caliche causes three main problems for the roots of garden plants not adapted to it. First, naturally deep-rooted plants can't penetrate it. Second, it slows drainage, causing water to collect and drown roots. And third, when the trapped water evaporates it leaves behind salts, which poison the soil.

There are no magic chemicals you can add to the soil to dissolve caliche. But finding it in your garden doesn't mean you have to scrap your landscaping plans and install a patio instead!

⬥ *What can I do about caliche in my garden?*

It depends on the kinds of plants you wish to grow.

If you want to put in non-desert plants, you have little choice but to remove caliche if it seriously impedes drainage. The test is to fill your planting holes with water. If they don't drain out in an hour or two, you have a problem.

If you're lucky, and the caliche is fairly light,

you may be able to remove it with a shovel. A heavier deposit may yield to the long pointed iron rod known affectionately as a "caliche bar." Working with this tool will test your perseverance. It may help to think of it as an extended upper body workout, a exercise in character building, or a productive way to vent frustrations. You may prefer to rent a jackhammer or hire a professional.

Raised beds are an alternative, but they won't be sufficient for deep-rooted trees. And of course neither raised beds nor caliche removal will be all that's required for non-desert plants, which tend

also to be unsuited to the desert's **alkaline,** nutrient-poor soils. You'll need to consider soil amendments and fertilizers as well.

♦ *Do I need to remove caliche if I'm putting in desert plants?*

Good news: unless it's a heavy layer within a few inches of the surface, probably not! Caliche is, after all, a nearly ubiquitous phenomenon in deserts, and many desert plants are adapted to it. Their roots lie close to the surface, often above any limy deposits. They need little moisture, so if you avoid the pitfalls of overwatering (see

THE CALICHE MYSTERY: THE ANSWER WAS BLOWING IN THE WIND

For years the origin of the limy, calcium-rich soil deposits called **caliche** was a puzzle. Where does the calcium come from? The most obvious answer, that it simply dissolves out of the soil's rock ingredients, clearly didn't work. Caliche occurs without regard to the soil's "parent materials," even in soils derived from calcium-poor volcanic rock. It's as though the calcium comes out of thin air.

In fact, that's almost what happens. It's now believed that the calcium in caliche arrives in two ways: as airborne dust particles, and dissolved in raindrops. Its ultimate origin may be in limestone deposits, dry lakebeds, and evaporating ocean spray hundreds or even thousands of miles away!

When rain falls in the desert, the calcium it brings with it mixes with what it dissolves from the dust on the soil surface. The calcium is carried downward as far as the rainwater penetrates. Carbon dioxide breathed out by plant roots helps complete a chemical reaction creating calcium carbonate, which is deposited as the soil dries. Caliche is found in deserts all around the world, but in rainy climates the calcium is simply washed on down into the groundwater, so the soil remains caliche-free.

Since its major constituent is imported so slowly, caliche takes a very long time to form. Even threadlike veins and small nodules may take several thousand years to appear. A thick, thoroughly cemented layer probably began to form more than 100,000 years ago, well back into the **Pleistocene period** (the Ice Ages), long before human beings set foot in the Southwest.

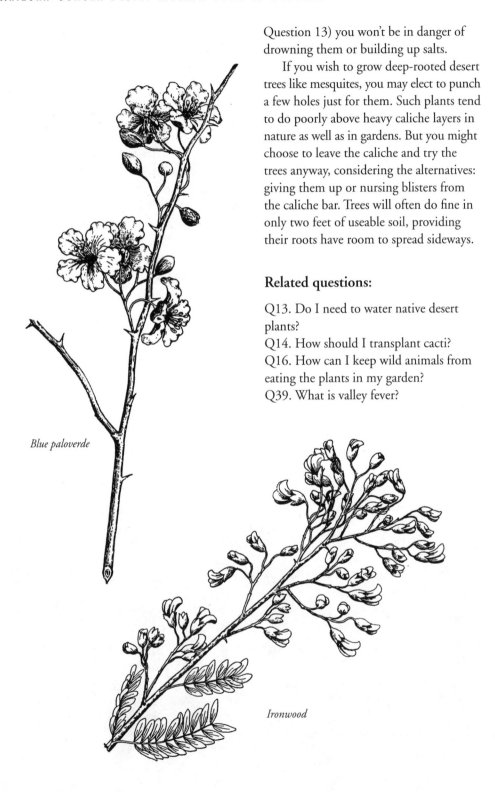

Question 13) you won't be in danger of drowning them or building up salts.

If you wish to grow deep-rooted desert trees like mesquites, you may elect to punch a few holes just for them. Such plants tend to do poorly above heavy caliche layers in nature as well as in gardens. But you might choose to leave the caliche and try the trees anyway, considering the alternatives: giving them up or nursing blisters from the caliche bar. Trees will often do fine in only two feet of useable soil, providing their roots have room to spread sideways.

Related questions:

Q13. Do I need to water native desert plants?
Q14. How should I transplant cacti?
Q16. How can I keep wild animals from eating the plants in my garden?
Q39. What is valley fever?

Blue paloverde

Ironwood

How can I keep wild animals from eating the plants in my garden?

ANSWER: *You can avoid attracting the creatures or you can use physical barriers to keep them out.*

Let's look at both these approaches in turn, keeping in mind that a combination of measures may work best in your particular situation.

♦ How can I avoid attracting problem animals to my garden?

• First, don't feed them! Obviously, deliberately feeding desert animals is offering them an open invitation to the premises, but so is feeding them inadvertently by putting out an uncovered garbage container or a dish of pet food.

Many desert mammals are attracted by birdseed spilled on the ground from feeders, so choose a feeder that's spill proof, or, if you broadcast seed, put out only a handful at a time. These precautions will also help prevent spreading bird diseases. (See Question 19.)

• Second, don't put in a pond or watering hole. This can be as much an "attractive nuisance" as food, and it, too, can spread disease. (Again, see Question 19.)

• Third, learn which plants will and won't be eaten. Ask other gardeners about their experiences and experiment on your own. Here's a start: strong-smelling and very spiny plants tend to be left alone. You'll probably have the best results if you avoid exotic plants and put in native species. They're likely to have evolved defenses against native **herbivores**.

• Fourth, don't create a lush oasis by your landscaping. Dense vegetation will draw animals with the promise of food and moisture as well as shade and hiding places. The temptation to desert creatures is strongest during droughts, and you can minimize it at those times by not watering your desert plants. Be especially sure not to overwater—it may make your plants irresistibly tender and tasty. (See Question 13.)

Rock squirrel

• Fifth, talk to your neighbors. Your own efforts will be of little avail if your garden becomes a stop on the javelina highway to an all-they-can-eat restaurant next door.

◆ What barriers work to exclude problem wildlife?

Javelina can be kept out with a solid wall or a strong mesh fence. It need not be very tall—javelina usually won't jump over a two-foot barrier. They will try to burrow beneath a fence, though, so bury the base eight inches deep. Even better, bend the base outward (away from your yard) to form an apron two to three feet wide, then bury that.

A small area can be protected from javelina by a low-voltage electric fence with a single strand about ten inches above the ground. It won't injure the animals. Incidentally, spicy concoctions sprayed on plants seldom deter javelina.

Like javelina, jackrabbits and cottontails can be excluded by a solid wall or a mesh fence, though the openings in a standard chain-link fence are too large to keep out cottontails. You'll need a one-inch mesh for that. Again, burying the base of the fence helps. You can also put small-mesh cages around tender, newly installed landscape plants.

There's no humane and legal way to keep rock squirrels or small ground squirrels out of your garden, but it works to cage individual plants. You'll have to include lids on the cages, though.

Finally, when you find only a nipped-off stem where your favorite plant once stood, it may help to take a deep breath and remind yourself that the desert animals were here first. After all, we took something from them when we built our homes in their habitat. How annoyed should we be when they take a little something back?

Related questions:

Q10. Is a javelina a pig?
Q13. Do I need to water native desert plants?
Q17. How can I attract desert wildlife to my yard?
Q19. Don't birds sometimes catch a disease at feeders and birdbaths?
Q26. How can I keep rattlesnakes out of my yard?

Poultry netting protects vulnerable plants.

How can I attract desert wildlife to my yard?

ANSWER: *You can easily attract desert wildlife by providing food, water, and plant cover, but it's important not to overdo it.*

Because the desert is dry, its plant and animal life is naturally sparse. If you encourage desert animals to gather in unnatural numbers the result can be problems both for them and for yourself. But if you exercise common sense and restraint, attracting a few desert creatures to our homes can be a harmless source of enjoyment.

◆ *What are some of the pitfalls I should avoid?*

Don't put out an abundant supply of birdseed. It may attract destructive numbers of javelina, rabbits and squirrels,

BUTTERFLY GARDENING

Gardening for butterflies yields a double return on your investment—colorful flowers, and colorful insects, too. How to choose your plants? Limited published help is available, but you can always consult the experts: the butterflies themselves. Visit a nursery and watch which plants are being visited by butterflies. Explore your desert surroundings, too. If a promising native plant isn't commercially available, you may be able to collect wild seed and grow it yourself.

Put your butterfly plants in a sunny location and keep them pesticide-free. True enthusiasts don't limit their gardening to adult butterflies, but provide food plants for their larvae (caterpillars) as well. Why stop there? Find a good magnifying glass and enjoy the aphids, beetles, and all the other miniature creatures that make your garden their home.

and it may spread disease among the birds. The same goes for providing large quantities of water in the form of a pond or water hole. (See Question 19.)

Don't try to attract large mammals, especially javelina, by feeding them. If they're in the area they'll probably show up in your yard anyway. You may welcome an occasional visit, but if they make it a habit and tear up your plants, your attitude is likely to change. If they also tear up your neighbor's plants, his or her attitude is likely to change, too! (See Question 16.)

◆ *What works?*

Think small.

Instead of providing a constant, abundant supply of birdseed, try scattering just a handful at breakfast or dinner—natural feeding times for desert animals as well as for people, and convenient times for you to be watching. The animals will quickly learn the routine.

Instead of an abundant water supply, try a slow drip system, with the water falling into a small dish or onto a stone. Even an emitter from a drip irrigation system will be frequented by desert wildlife.

Instead of trying to attract large mammals, encourage smaller forms of wildlife with a variety of native plantings. Desert trees will provide sites for nesting birds, and the mistletoe growing in the trees will produce berries for them to eat. Smaller shrubs will supply cover and food for birds and small ground squirrels, and a good-sized cholla may attract a nesting pair of cactus wrens or thrashers. Certain specialized plants will bring in hummingbirds. (See Question 18.)

Keep in mind other habitat needs as well. A few sunny boulders and wooden fenceposts will provide habitat for lizards. You'll enjoy watching them bask, feed, and defend their territories. Undisturbed anthills will feed horned lizards. In fact, enjoy the ants and other insects, too! Gardening for butterflies can be especially rewarding. (See sidebar, previous page.)

And, especially, don't be obsessive about neatness. Wildlife gardening is a great excuse to relax your standards!

*Rule of thumb: native plants are often best for attracting native wildlife. They're more familiar to the animals than **exotic** garden plants, and they tend to be more resistant to being completely consumed.*

A brush pile, some leaf litter, and even a few weeds will attract insects and the birds and lizards that eat them.

The key is not to think of all this as something you do for the animals; they can get along without your help. Think of it as something you do for yourself, to bring just a few more animals to your home so you can enjoy watching and learning from them.

Related questions:

Q10. Is a javelina a pig?
Q13. Do I need to water native desert plants?
Q16. How can I keep wild animals from eating the plants in my garden?
Q18. How can I attract hummingbirds?
Q19. Don't birds sometimes catch a disease at feeders and birdbaths?
Q20. What should I do about an injured, sick, or orphaned animal in my yard?
Q29. How can I protect my pets from coyotes and bobcats?

Mourning dove

QUESTION
18

How can I attract hummingbirds?

ANSWER: *The easiest way is to put out a feeder.*

Hummingbirds are nectar-feeders, of course, so hummingbird feeders are simply artificial flowers filled with artificial nectar. Almost any commercially available hummingbird feeder will do, or you can improvise one yourself from a small container (say, a film can) painted red and hung from a wire. To make the nectar, dissolve one part table sugar in four parts water, boil it for a minute or two to sterilize it, then let it cool. After filling the feeder, hang it in a shady place, out of the wind. You can store any left-over solution in your refrigerator.

Unfortunately, besides being hummingbird ambrosia, sugar water is an excellent medium for growing bacteria, fungi, and other microorganisms. To prevent harm to the birds it's important to clean and refill your feeder at least once per week—twice that often in warm weather. Use a mild bleach solution (one part bleach to ten parts water) and rinse the feeder well afterward. A small bottle brush may help.

♦ Should I add red food coloring to the sugar water in my feeder?

While it's true that red attracts hummers (see sidebar, next page), food coloring isn't necessary because most feeders display red in their designs. Besides, while the red dye may be harmless to humans in small quantities, we can't be sure it's safe for hummingbirds in the huge amounts they might swallow at a feeder. A hummer may drink more than eight times its weight in nectar in a single day!

Incidentally, even that's not all a hummingbird consumes. Nectar is merely a high-carbohydrate energy food. Hummingbirds also eat many tiny insects and spiders, which provide needed salts, proteins and fats. The hummers in your yard will take care of that part of their diet themselves.

♦ What if no hummingbirds come to my feeder?

Hummingbirds are curious creatures and constantly explore their environment. If there are hummers in your neighborhood chances are they'll find your feeder. If after a few days you still have no takers, try making the feeder more conspicuous. Temporarily taping a red ribbon to it may help. If that doesn't work, try putting the feeder in a more visible spot. Once the birds have noticed it, you can move it a little every day until it's where you want it.

• What if other animals steal nectar from the feeder?

Larger birds such as orioles and woodpeckers may land on your feeder and tip out the nectar. If so, remove any built-in perches, or check with a dealer about a different feeder; some feeders are specially designed to thwart nuisance birds.

You can also tempt away other birds with a more convenient nectar source placed elsewhere—a wide-mouthed jar hung from a stout wire may work. If nocturnal animals raid your feeder, just take it down at night. The hummingbirds will be asleep.

Insects are often the most troublesome nectar thieves. A ring of petroleum jelly around the feeder's hanger will keep out ants. Bees and wasps can be blocked by plastic screening over the nectar ports, but be sure that the openings are large enough (at least $1/16$ inch) for a hummer's bill.

• What times of year should I put out my feeder?

There are hummingbirds in the Sonoran Desert in every season, so you can keep your feeder out year-round. And don't worry about the easy food keeping hummers from migrating—they'll usually depart anyway when the time comes.

SEEING RED

Have you ever been startled by a hummingbird investigating a bright red article of clothing? Hummingbirds are so strongly drawn to red objects that biologists once believed hummers had an innate predilection for that color. Experiments have now shown that newly hatched hummingbirds have no particular

Fairy duster

color preference. Instead, the powerful attraction of red for hummers is a learned association arising from many encounters with nectar-rich red "hummingbird flowers."

Such flowers have **coevolved** with hummingbirds and have become specialized for hummingbird **pollination**. Their warm colors—most often red, but sometimes orange or yellow—signal hummingbirds that the flowers contain abundant sweet nectar, the "fast food" that powers a hummer's highly energetic lifestyle. Since most insects can't see the color red, such flowers tend to be inconspicuous to these potential nectar thieves. And the tubular shapes of many hummingbird flowers exclude large insects but are just right for slender hummingbird bills.

If you go away on vacation, don't be concerned. An empty or missing feeder may cause regular visitors to abandon your yard, but they'll find food elsewhere. Remember, you're feeding the birds for your own sake—so you can have the pleasure of observing them at your home. They can do fine without your help.

✦ Is that all there is to it?

That depends on you. You may become so fascinated by these colorful and pugnacious creatures that eventually you'll want to go beyond artificial feeders and offer the birds water for bathing as well as natural nectar sources. Some of the references listed in the bibliography will help you start your own desert hummingbird garden.

Related questions:

Q17. How can I attract desert wildlife to my yard?
See also Appendix B: Hummingbird Gardens.

QUESTION
19

Don't birds sometimes catch a disease at feeders and birdbaths?

ANSWER: *You're probably thinking of trichomoniasis.*

Trichomoniasis (trik-uh-muh-NY-uh-sis) in birds is caused by the protozoan *Trichomonas gallinae.* The disease has been known for centuries to people who rear feathered animals. Pigeon fanciers call it "canker;" falconers call it "frounce." (Trichomoniasis in humans is caused by a different microorganism. People can't catch trichomoniasis from birds, nor vice-versa.)

Trich usually infects a bird's mouth and throat, but it can spread widely through the body. It harms mostly young birds, but adults can be symptomless carriers. An infected bird may seem listless, emaciated, and unkempt —but it also may appear quite healthy. In severe cases it will usually have a cheesy material in its throat that can seriously interfere with swallowing and breathing.

Trich is most prevalent in pigeons and doves. In this zoological family, courting birds share the protozoan when they rub their beaks together—a behavior called "billing." They later infect their young when they feed them a regurgitated liquid called **crop milk**. Pigeons and doves may also spread trich by dropping seeds they're unable to swallow, and drinking (or trying to) at bird baths. The disease usually stays at low levels in pigeon and dove populations, but sometimes there are outbreaks (**epizootics**) during which many birds die.

Raptors like hawks and owls can be badly infected as nestlings when their

HOW (AN I STOP BIRDS FROM FLYING INTO MY WINDOW?

Reflections in windows—especially inviting images of plant-filled landscapes and open sky—are a kind of virtual reality with unfortunate consequences for birds. Here are some things to try.

A paper cut-out of a flying raptor will deter smaller birds from colliding with your picture window.

- Avoid enhancing the illusion with reflective window films.
- Don't place a feeder or birdbath near a picture window.
- Attach a silhouette of a flying falcon to the window. You can buy one at a nature store or cut one out yourself.
- Hang objects outside the window. Strips of plastic or foil work, but you might like to try something more attractive—say, macrame, wind socks, or a shiny mobile.

parents feed them diseased prey. Much less is known about how frequently other desert birds are infected.

• Are there other diseases in backyard desert birds?

Unfortunately, yes. For example: *Salmonellosis* is caused by bacteria spread through bird droppings—sometimes at feeders. It's often fatal.

Aspergillosis is caused by fungi that can grow in damp bird seed and in debris under feeders. Birds are infected when they inhale the fungal spores or eat moldy food.

Avian pox is caused by a virus spread by direct contact between birds and through feeders and insects. It causes wartlike growths.

• How can I feed birds without spreading disease?

Crowding helps spread disease in backyard birds. Not only does it encourage transmission, it also can stress birds, making them more susceptible.

If you use a feeder, avoid any in which the birds can walk through the seed. Look for a model that's spill-proof, to avoid crowds of birds on the ground. (Spilled birdseed can attract problem animals, too—see Questions 21 and 29.) Sweep or hose off the area under the feeder daily and clean out the feeder whenever you refill it. It helps to sterilize it with a 10% bleach solution (1 part bleach to 9 parts water).

If you throw birdseed on the ground, take only a small handful—no more than the birds will eat in about fifteen minutes—and broadcast it in a sunny area of several square yards. Do this only once a day, at a time when you can enjoy watching the birds—perhaps at breakfast or dinner, which are natural feeding times for them, too. Sweep or hose off the area between feedings, rotate feeding areas, or both.

> *Diseases can be a problem for backyard birds, but many more birds are killed by cats or by flying into picture windows.*

Store birdseed in a waterproof and rodent-proof container, and discard any that's damp, musty-smelling, or visibly spoiled.

• How can I provide water for birds without spreading disease?

Some disease organisms survive well in standing water, so it's safer to use a device that drips water onto a stone or into a shallow dish. Nature stores carry these, or you can make one yourself with an ordinary drip irrigation emitter. Hose off the area occasionally to keep it clean.

If you prefer a birdbath, choose a shallow basin and place it in direct sunlight. (Heat and **ultraviolet** light kill some pathogens.) Clean it out daily and let it dry in the sun before refilling. It's a good idea also to scrub it once a week with a 10% bleach solution. Always wash your hands after handling the container.

Place the birdbath in an open area where cats can't hide, but not near a feeder—that would encourage crowding.

Ground-level watering holes and ponds are much more difficult to keep clean, and also more likely to attract problem wildlife. (See Question 16.)

• Given the possibility of spreading disease, wouldn't it be better not to give seed or water to wild birds?

Many people have come to that conclusion. They point out that the very safest way to attract a variety of birds is with bird-friendly landscaping. Some of the references listed in the bibliography can help you choose plants that provide birds with nesting sites, hiding places, and food.

Still, feeding and watering seem to be reasonably safe—as long as you're careful. If you suspect a year-round commitment to regular cleaning might be hard to keep, it makes sense to stick to low-maintenance methods: a modest dripper and an occasional handful of seed flung on the ground.

Remember, the birds can get along just fine without our help. If we attract them for our own pleasure, we owe it to them to keep our backyards safe.

Related questions:

Q16. How can I keep wild animals from eating the plants in my garden?
Q17. How can I attract desert wildlife to my yard?
Q18. How can I attract hummingbirds?
Q20. What should I do about an injured, sick, or orphaned animal in my yard?

What should I do about an injured, sick, or orphaned animal in my yard?

ANSWER: *First you must decide whether or not to get involved.*

This isn't always easy. On the one hand, there's the reasonable view that nature should be allowed to take its course. On the other hand, a distressed animal in your yard may not be a "natural" situation; for example, it may have been injured by a neighborhood cat. And it's hard to let an animal suffer.

Caring for an injured animal takes a special commitment of time and patience.

If you decide to take action, there are limits to what you should do yourself, to avoid harming both the animal and you. There are also legal restrictions to the "possession" of wildlife, which includes having wild animals in your care. Do only what's reasonable—see below—and

if more is needed, let a licensed wildlife rehabilitator take it from there.

Your community may have a central phone number for a wildlife rehabilitation organization—check the yellow pages under "wildlife." If not, call a local nature center, zoo, or the nearest office of your state's fish and game department. (See the organizations list at the back of this book.) They can refer you.

• *How much should I do myself?*

Here's how to handle the most common situations. If you need to put the animal in a box for transportation to a licensed wildlife rehabilitator, see the sidebar on the next page for details. Good luck!

Helpless baby bird fallen from nest. Put the bird back in the nest. If the whole nest has fallen, tie or wire it back in the tree. Act quickly: an exposed nestling is quite susceptible to excessive heat or cold. If you can't find the nest, place the bird gently in a box and call a licensed wildlife rehabilitator right away. Some baby birds need to be fed every half hour.

You may have heard that the odor of a human being will prevent a parent bird from accepting its young. Not true. Most birds have poor senses of smell and will readily accept progeny you've handled.

Abandoned, well-feathered young bird on the ground. Make sure it's really abandoned! Young birds of many species leave the nest before they're fully able to fly, and the parents continue caring for them. There's an excellent chance your bird's parents are off gathering food and will return if you give them a chance.

Keep pets and children away from the bird and observe it from a distance for an hour (or longer for a dove). If no parent shows up, catch the bird, put it in a box, and call a licensed wildlife rehabilitator.

Injured or sick adult bird. To avoid being hurt by the bird's beak or claws, handle it with gloves. If the bird is difficult to catch, try tossing a towel or box over it. Put the patient in a box and call a licensed wildlife rehabilitator.

If it's a large **raptor**, a predatory bird with a sharp beak and talons, don't try to capture it yourself. You could very easily get hurt. Just call for help.

Abandoned, injured, or sick baby cottontails. Mother cottontails visit their young only a few times during the night, so if you come across an unattended nest of tiny babies, don't worry—they're probably fine. If the nest has been disturbed, it's okay to put the babies back and cover it up. A healthy-looking older baby (eyes open) alone in the desert is no cause for concern, either. But if you find an obviously injured or sick young cottontail, pick it up with gloves, put it in a box, and call a licensed wildlife rehabilitator.

WILDLIFE TRAVEL TIPS

Being kept in a box for transportation to a wildlife rehabilitator is stressful for an animal, but you can minimize the stress.

1. Reduce the length of time you handle the animal by preparing the container in advance. Choose a cardboard box with enough room for the creature to stand and turn around, punch holes in the sides or top, and line the bottom with paper towels or soft cloth.

2. Once the animal is in the box, put it in a warm (not hot), dark, and quiet place, and avoid disturbing the patient by frequently peeking at it.

3. Don't give the animal anything to eat or drink unless you're advised to do so by a wildlife professional or a licensed wildlife rehabilitator.

Caring for abandoned, injured, or sick wildlife is like rearing a child: it requires long hours, patience, and a willingness often to subordinate one's own needs to those of another living thing. Licensed wildlife rehabilitators are thoroughly trained and have both state and federal permits to do their work. They don't charge for their services (but they often welcome donations). Don't hesitate to call them.

Incidentally, though you're unlikely to find one in your yard, an "abandoned" deer fawn is usually being cared for by its mother, too. (See Question 41.)

• Other distressed mammals

Don't capture or handle other young or adult mammals unless advised to do so by a wildlife professional or a licensed wildlife rehabilitator. Other mammals are much more likely to injure you or themselves. Some carry diseases you can catch, and so do their fleas.

Another consideration: unlike most birds, most mammals *do* have strong

senses of smell, so unnecessarily handled babies may be rejected by their parents. If they must be reared in captivity they may never again be able to live in the wild.

• How can I protect neighborhood wildlife?

• Avoid drawing wildlife crowds to your yard by offering too much food or water. You could attract problem animals and spread disease. (See Questions 16, 17, and 19.)

• Keep your cat indoors and don't let your dog roam free. (See Question 29 sidebar, page 88.)

• Never try to make a wild animal a pet. Domestic animals have been bred for many generations to live well with humans, but captivity is stressful and unhealthy for most wild animals. And captive wildlife can be dangerous and illegal for you.

• Teach children why small wild animals should be left alone, no matter how "cute" and harmless they may seem.

Related questions:

Q16. How can I keep wild animals from eating the plants in my garden?
Q17. How can I attract desert wildlife to my yard?
Q19. Don't birds sometimes catch a disease at feeders and birdbaths?
Q29. How can I protect my pets from coyotes and bobcats? (sidebar, page 88)
See also Appendix D: Hantavirus.

How should I identify bark scorpions, black widows, and brown spiders?

ANSWER: *Carefully.*

Just kidding. But while these interesting **arachnids** aren't the fearsome creatures many people have been led to believe, it is true they can be dangerous under the right circumstances. (See sidebar, page 67.) It's an excellent idea to learn how to recognize them.

If you have the misfortune to be stung or bitten, you'll find first aid advice in Appendix C.

BARK SCORPION
(*Centruroides exilicauda*)

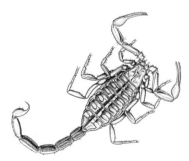

Bark scorpion

Other names: Slender scorpion. Some older references use the scientific name *Centruroides sculpturatus.*

Identification: A small scorpion, up to 1½ inches long, usually straw colored. *The pincers and tail are noticeably more slender than in other Sonoran Desert scorpions,* such as the stripe-tailed scorpion with which it's often confused.

Stripe-tailed scorpion

Where found: Bark scorpions are climbers and most common around trees, especially near streams and washes—though they live in many other habitats, too. They're active at night, but often found by day hanging onto the undersides of rocks, fallen branches, boards, and bits of bark. They also show up indoors, especially (but not only) in new developments where their natural habitat has recently been disturbed.

BLACK WIDOW SPIDER
(*Latrodectus hesperus*)

Black widow spider

Besides spiders and scorpions, a host of more exotic arachnids thrive in the Sonoran Desert's warm climate. Known by such names as solpugids, vinegaroons, pseudoscorpions, and harvestmen, a few may be alarming in appearance, but none are dangerous, and all are intriguing. It's worth spending some time with a field guide to get acquainted.

Other names: Some scientists prefer to use the name "black widow" only for the eastern species *Latrodectus mactans.* They call related species simply "widow spiders."

Identification: An adult female is shiny black or dark brown and about an inch and a half across, including the legs. She has a *globe-shaped abdomen about ½ inch across with a conspicuous red hourglass pattern on the underside.* A juvenile female is smaller, with a cream-colored hourglass; she also has red, brown, and cream markings on top of her abdomen. Males are harmless and very small. Their bodies are less than ¼ inch long and marked like young females, though they lack the globular abdomen.

Where found: Black widows are more common around buildings than in undisturbed desert. Females make large, shapeless webs near the ground in protected nooks and crannies, especially in garages, outbuildings, and woodpiles. They stay out of sight during the day, and at night they hang upside-down in their webs, displaying their hourglasses. In the desert, webs are in rodent burrows, debris, rocky niches, and other protected places.

BROWN SPIDERS
(*Loxosceles* species)

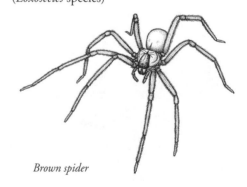

Brown spider

Other names: People often use the name "brown recluse" for Sonoran Desert members of the genus *Loxosceles,* but the true (and more dangerous) brown recluse spider, *Loxosceles reclusa,* lives in the

JUST HOW DANGEROUS ARE BARK SCORPIONS, BLACK WIDOWS, AND BROWN SPIDERS?

Not as dangerous as you might think. While all three are potentially life-threatening under certain specific circumstances—mainly involving the very young, the very old, and people with compromised health—deaths from scorpion stings and spider bites are *extremely* rare in the United States. If you've been stung or bitten by one of these creatures, or think you may have been, call a physician or your local poison control center for advice. (For more information about symptoms and treatments, see Appendix C.)

Venom is expensive for an animal to manufacture. It's used mainly for subduing prey, and often for starting digestion. No spider or scorpion—or venomous reptile, for that matter—is eager to spend this valuable fluid on something as large and unappetizing as a human being! Instead, scorpions and spiders hide or flee if they can. They usually sting or bite only if they're trapped or pressed against the skin.

(However, black widows sometimes bite a hand or foot that's dangled in their web, mistaking it for prey; and yes, it's true, something similar can happen to men and boys in outhouses.)

Few desert dwellers are ever stung by scorpions or bitten by black widows or brown spiders. If you're one of the lucky ones, you'll almost certainly live to tell the tale!

Midwest and Southeast. All such spiders sometimes go by the more colorful names "violin spider" and "fiddleback spider."

Identification: It's difficult. An adult brown spider is about an inch across counting the legs, smooth looking (not hairy or spiny), and tan to brown with unbanded legs and a darker upside-down *violin-shaped marking on the front of the body*. Unfortunately, the violin is hard to see, and there are many other brown-colored spiders, some with similar markings. Specialists count the eyes with a magnifier: brown spiders have six, while other similar spiders have eight. You may be able to do this, too—once the spider is safely in a jar!

Where found: Brown spiders are nocturnal. Outdoors they can be found by day under rocks and bits of wood or in packrat nests, clinging to sticky, white, irregularly-shaped mats of silk. Indoors they're usually on the ground (not hanging in webs) in dark closets and corners, but sometimes they conceal themselves in bedding or clothing. (See Question 22.)

Related questions:

Q22. How can I keep dangerous scorpions and spiders out of my house?
See also Appendix C: Venomous Bites and Stings.

QUESTION 22

How can I keep dangerous scorpions and spiders out of my house?

ANSWER: *Don't leave them any way to get in.*

Bark scorpions, black widows, and brown spiders are fascinating creatures, but it's perfectly reasonable not to want them as housemates! Start by installing good weather stripping around doors and windows. Then make an inspection tour of the outside of your house, sealing up every crack and crevice that could be an entryway. Openings needed for ventilation can be covered with screening.

All this will be of little avail if you inadvertently smuggle in the creatures yourself—for example, by failing to inspect a box before bringing it in from an outdoor storage shed. Special case: people sometimes carry home brown spiders in attractive bits of cholla cactus skeleton they pick up in the desert.

• *What should I do about the scorpions and spiders I find indoors?*

Few people would fault you for summarily dispatching a dangerous scorpion or spider with a fly swatter, but consider the alternatives. If you're not too afraid, you may be able carefully to scoop up the creature in a jar and relocate it outdoors.

The animal may be out of place in your home, but it has significant ecological roles to play in the desert, both as predator and as prey.

If you're a parent, consider the lessons your actions give to your children. A fearful reaction in an adult teaches a child to be fearful, too; but making the effort to deal with a spider or scorpion without killing it teaches a respect for all living things. Besides, the opportunity to see the

WHAT ABOUT PESTICIDES?

Pesticides tend to be ineffective in controlling spiders and scorpions, and many people prefer to avoid these chemicals because of the harm they can do to other animals—including ourselves. If you feel you must use pesticides, consult your county's Cooperative Extension office beforehand. (See the organizations list at the back of this book.) Be sure to follow all directions very carefully, and of course keep the containers well out of the reach of children.

captive animal up close will help the child learn both how to recognize it and how interesting it is.

Of course, releasing your venomous visitor in your neighbor's yard would teach your child an unfortunate lesson of quite another kind!

• What about the indoor spiders and scorpions I haven't found?

A thorough housecleaning and domestic clutter reduction program will both uncover hidden houseguests and make your home less hospitable to them. There are also certain specific things you can do about the three animals of greatest concern.

BARK SCORPION

Buy or borrow a portable blacklight (an **ultraviolet** lamp) and go on a nighttime scorpion hunt. The **exoskeletons** of all scorpions (except newborns) glow green under UV light, making them easy to find. If this rather spooky procedure doesn't appeal to you, "sticky traps" can also be quite effective. You can buy them from do-it-yourself pest control companies and at hardware stores. But don't use sticky traps outdoors—they can trap other things, too.

Until you've solved your bark scorpion problem, put the legs of your bed or your child's crib in glass jars, which are too slippery for scorpion feet to negotiate. Inspect bedding before retiring, and shake out your clothing and shoes in the morning, cowboy style.

BLACK WIDOW SPIDER

Black widows aren't often found inside modern houses, but it can happen. They do show up frequently in nooks and crannies

around buildings outdoors, as well as in storage sheds and garages. Check likely living places with a flashlight after dark, when the large females will be hanging conspicuously in the centers of their webs. It also helps to remove any of the silken egg sacs you may find in the webs.

When working in areas where black widows are likely to be, you can protect yourself with long sleeves and gloves.

BROWN SPIDERS

Housecleaning is the best approach, paying special attention to the dark and protected spots favored by the species. Vacuum cleaners do a good job of eliminating small spiders you're unlikely to see.

Until you're quite sure your house is brown-spider-free, check your bedding before retiring, and inspect clothing before putting it on. Brown spiders sometimes hide in these places, and most people are bitten while getting into bed or getting dressed.

Other than black widows and brown spiders, any spiders you find in your house will almost certainly be harmless, as well as allies against unwanted insects. Incidentally, tarantulas seldom get inside houses, and they aren't dangerous, anyway. (See Question 37, sidebar, page 114.)

• Would it help to eliminate the scorpions and spiders in my yard?

If you've been thorough about sealing the entryways, it would be hard for spiders and scorpions to find their way back indoors. Still, if you've had a serious problem in the past you might want to reduce the outdoor reservoir of potential invaders. Boards lying on the ground and piles of wood, stones, and other objects

all provide **microhabitats** for scorpions and spiders, as well as for their prey. To be safe, wear leather gloves while cleaning these things up.

It would be impossible to eliminate all the scorpions and spiders in your yard forever, so rather than engaging in an endless war against these desert natives, why not declare a truce with those that remain? Outdoors, they're not likely to hurt you, and for all you know they're helping to control problem insects around your home. You might even find these much-maligned creatures interesting once you get to know them.

Of course, if you have young children it makes sense to keep an area as free of dangerous critters as possible, so the kids can play safely outdoors. For more about such "safe areas," see Question 26.

Related questions:

Q21. How should I identify bark scorpions, black widows, and brown spiders?
Q23. How can I tell if the bees in my yard are Africanized?
Q26. How can I keep rattlesnakes out of my yard?
Q28. Why do packrats keep making houses in my car's engine compartment?
Q37. How can I avoid dangerous encounters with rattlers and Gila monsters? (See sidebar, page 113.)
See also Appendix C: Venomous Bites and Stings.

QUESTION

How can I tell if the bees in my yard are Africanized?

ANSWER: *You usually can't. African-ized bees look almost exactly like other honey bees.*

Africanized bees closely resemble the other honey bees in North America because they're just different races of the same species: *Apis mellifera.* Even experts have to make careful measurements to tell them apart. The most important—and interesting—differences are in their behavior. (See sidebar, next page.)

Africanized or not, a few foraging honey bees are usually no cause for alarm. Unless you're allergic to bee stings, the only true danger is near an Africanized colony. (See Question 24.)

◆ *How can I keep Africanized bees from colonizing my house or yard?*

By eliminating potential nesting places.

To discourage honey bees (of any kind) from taking up residence in your house, close off their entryways. Cover or caulk any holes or cracks more than ⅛ inch wide in the foundation, walls, and roof, and screen off drains and vents.

To discourage bees from squatting in your yard, remove any debris that could give them shelter—tires, auto parts, old appliances, boxes, overturned flower pots. Screen or cover openings in water valve boxes, keep shed doors tightly closed, and plug holes in trees.

Africanized bees are less choosy about their nest sites than other honey bees, and they'll move into smaller spaces. Taking the above advice won't completely bee-proof your home, but if you hope to avoid unwanted guests there's no point in issuing unnecessary invitations.

If you're very concerned, or if you've had repeated problems with bee colonies, traps baited with special honey bee odors, or **pheromones**, are available from some beekeepers and pest control companies.

◆ *What else can I do to stay safe from Africanized bees around my home?*

Africanized bees are already common in some Sonoran Desert cities, but if you're aware of your surroundings and use common sense you have very little to fear.

Keep an eye out for colonies in your neighborhood. Look for large numbers of bees flying in and out of an opening. If you find a colony, warn your neighbors. Don't approach it or try to remove it

OUT OF AFRICA: AN ECOLOGICAL CLIFFHANGER

The story of the honey bee in the Americas is a fascinating one, and one of its most interesting chapters is being written right now.

A few hundred years ago there were no honey bees in the New World, though there were many native bees of other kinds. The first honey bees arrived with European settlers in the sixteenth century. These valued insects had been bred to be docile, and were well adapted to temperate climates. They formed large colonies in well-insulated cavities, stockpiled honey for the long winters, and seldom relinquished these investments by abandoning their hives ("absconding").

European bees thrived in North America, and they live today in managed hives and **feral** colonies all across the continent. But they never did well in the American tropics.

In 1956 a Brazilian geneticist imported some honey bees from Africa in the hope of breeding a bee more suited to South and Central America. The African bees behaved very differently from their European relatives. In their warm tropical homelands they had been frequently raided by predators (including honey-seeking humans) and subjected to unpredictable scarcity of the flowers they visited. They had adapted by stockpiling less honey, making smaller colonies, defending them vigorously, and often absconding to seek better conditions.

Unfortunately, some of the bees soon escaped. They reproduced rapidly and spread quickly through South and Central America, displacing European bees in managed hives and establishing numerous feral colonies. They reached Texas in 1990 and crossed the border into Arizona and California a few years later.

How far north will these tropical bees be able to spread? To what extent will they hybridize with European honey bees? How will they change the beekeeping industry? How well will they adapt to desert habitats? How seriously will they affect the Sonoran Desert's native bees and the plants they pollinate? Stay tuned.

---

yourself. Call a beekeeper or pest control company.

People are understandably frightened when they find a large cluster of honey bees hanging on a tree limb. This probably isn't a colony, but a swarm searching for a new nest site. Swarming bees aren't usually very defensive, but be careful anyway. Treat a swarm just like a hive.

Check around your home for colonies just before running equipment such as power tools, weed eaters, and lawn mowers.

Africanized bee colonies may respond to the noise as well as the smell. And never tether a pet near a possible nest.

Related questions:

Q22. How can I keep dangerous scorpions and spiders out of my house?
Q24. How dangerous are Africanized bees?
Q31. What precautions should I take when hiking in the desert?

QUESTION
24

How dangerous are Africanized bees?

ANSWER: *Africanized bees are more dangerous than other honey bees only when they're defending their nests.*

Despite the unfortunate moniker "killer bees," bestowed by overheated news media, Africanized bees don't seek out and attack people out of sheer orneriness. In fact, the whole notion of these insects as exceptionally *aggressive* is misleading; better to think of them as highly *defensive*, and then only concerning their nests.

An Africanized bee taking a drink or gathering nectar and pollen away from its nest is as unlikely to bother you as any other honey bee is. Even if you manage to

provoke it into stinging, say by stepping on it, its sting is no more dangerous. (Or no less dangerous: *any* honey bee sting is hazardous if you're allergic to it. See Appendix C.)

Swarms of Africanized bees looking for new places to colonize are usually innocuous, too. The bees tend to be so gorged with honey—provisions for the trip—that they'd have trouble stinging even if they were so inclined. But why take chances? Keep your distance.

The danger arises when you disturb well-established colonies. Africanized bees are much more sensitive than other honey bees to perceived threats to their nests. They're more likely to react, and they may react more quickly and in much larger numbers. Some Africanized bee colonies

> *A person in the United States has less chance of dying in an Africanized bee attack than of being struck by lightning.*

aren't very defensive, but others are. People and animals unable to escape severe defensive attacks have sometimes died as a result of multiple stings.

The bottom line? Statistically speaking, your chances of perishing in an Africanized bee attack are almost vanishingly small. On the other hand, if you happen to join the tiny minority of people who *are* attacked, you'll be in a potentially dangerous situation. It's worth knowing in advance how to respond.

◆ What should I do if I'm attacked?

You probably never will be, but if you are:

• *Run* immediately. *Don't hesitate* to retrieve belongings.

• As you run, *cover your face.* Pull your shirt up over your face, or use your hands.

• Keep running until you've escaped the bees (you may have to run as far as a quarter mile) or until you can *take shelter* in a building or an automobile.

• *Don't* flail your arms to fight off the bees. It won't help, and it may just rile them more.

• *Don't* try to escape underwater. The bees will still be there when you come up for air.

Once you're safe, remove any stingers as quickly as possible. Venom sacs will still be attached, pumping their contents into your skin, so the sooner the stingers come out, the better.

If you feel ill, think you might be allergic, or have been stung more than fifteen times, get medical attention immediately.

(For first aid for local swelling and discomfort caused by any bee sting, see Appendix C.)

• *Now that Africanized bees are here, wouldn't it be best just to kill all honey bees?*

Far from it. Not only are honey bees fascinating creatures and providers of honey, they're hugely important to us as pollinators. About a third of all the food we eat comes from plants pollinated by honey bees!

Beekeepers are already learning how to deal with the newcomers. For the rest of us, Africanized bees will become just one more of life's minor hazards—something to be aware of, but nothing to stop us from enjoying our backyards or the desert.

Related questions:

Q23. How can I tell if the bees in my yard are Africanized?
Q31. What precautions should I take when hiking in the desert?
See also Appendix C: Venomous Bites and Stings.

QUESTION
25

What kind of snake
is in my yard?

ANSWER: *We can tell you the most likely candidates.*

There are any number of possibilities —including your neighbor's escaped pet boa constrictor!—but certain kinds of snakes show up in Sonoran Desert backyards much more frequently than others. Check these descriptions first. If you don't recognize your legless visitor here, consult one of the excellent field guides listed in the bibliography.

RATTLESNAKES
(*Crotalus* species)

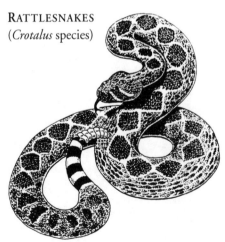

Western diamondback rattlesnake
Crotalus atrox

Forget what you may have heard about rattlesnakes having triangular heads—

some other desert snakes also fit that description. And forget about diamond-shaped markings—not all rattlesnakes have them and some other snakes do. Look (from a prudent distance) for the rattle.

If the snake has been born recently, the rattle will have just a single segment. If it's an older snake, some of the segments may have been lost. But the rattle will be there.

Consult a field guide if you'd like to identify the species—there are quite a few in the Sonoran Desert. For what to do about the rattlesnake in your yard, see Question 26.

GOPHER SNAKE
(*Pituophis melanoleucus*)

There are gopher snakes (sometimes called "bull snakes") all across North America, and they vary considerably in appearance. Those in the Sonoran Desert have a cream or yellowish ground color, large brown blotches on the back, and smaller blotches on the sides. They can be more than six feet long, though most are smaller.

Gopher snakes sometimes climb into plants to raid bird nests, but you're more likely to find one on the ground, especially where there are squirrel burrows and packrat nests. When cornered, these snakes sometimes do a very convincing (though probably unconscious) rattlesnake imitation. They coil, vibrate their tails, flatten their heads and hiss.

Gopher snake
Pituophis melanoleucus

Don't be fooled. Gopher snakes are quite harmless, and they're helpful to have around if rodents and rabbits are feasting on the plants in your garden.

COMMON KINGSNAKE
(*Lampropeltis getulus*)

This is another highly variable snake with a broad geographic range. In the Sonoran Desert of Arizona and California common kingsnakes are usually black

Common kingsnake
Lampropeltis getulus

with white or yellowish cross-bands. Less commonly in our region they may be all black, speckled, or even striped lengthwise. Check a field guide if you think you've found one of these forms.

Common kingsnakes eat rodents, birds, frogs and toads, lizards, and other snakes—including rattlesnakes. They sometimes vibrate their tails and strike if annoyed, much like gopher snakes, but they're harmless.

WHIPSNAKES
(*Masticophis* species)

These are all fast-moving snakes with slender, tapering, whiplike bodies. Three

Coachwhip
Masticophis flagellum

of the four species in our region—the Sonoran, striped, and California whipsnakes—have lengthwise stripes on their sides. The fourth, the coachwhip, is usually reddish with dark cross-bands on the neck, fading toward the rear of the snake, but some coachwhips (especially near Tucson) are solid black on the back, and there is almost every variation in between.

Whipsnakes eat rodents, birds, insects, lizards and snakes. When frightened, they retreat at lightning speed on the ground or escape into trees and bushes—they're very agile climbers. These snakes aren't venomous, but they often bite when caught.

WESTERN BLIND SNAKE
(*Leptotyphlops humilis*)

Just recognizing this as a snake is the hard part! Blind snakes are small—often

Western blind snake
Leptotyphlops humilis

less than a foot long—and look so much like shiny pink, purple, or brownish earthworms that they're sometimes called

"worm snakes." But unlike earthworms they have scales, vestigial eyes (two dark spots under the head scales) and a tiny spine on the tail—not to mention the backbones and other anatomical characteristics that make them the **vertebrates** that they are.

Blind snakes spend much of their time out of sight underground. Their shape and size allow them to enter narrow spaces in search of insect prey; they often invade the nests of ants and termites. Blind snakes sometimes come out at night, and you might come across one while you're digging in your garden.

Related questions:

Q26. How can I keep rattlesnakes out of my yard?
Q37. How can I avoid dangerous encounters with rattlers and Gila monsters?
Q38. Are there other venomous reptiles in the Sonoran Desert?

QUESTION

How can I keep rattlesnakes out of my yard?

ANSWER: *A low wall will keep out rattlesnakes—and most other snakes as well.*

Snakes can't climb smooth vertical surfaces, so an untextured wall makes an excellent barrier. It needn't be more than a yard tall to keep out most snakes. Avoid building any corners that are concave toward the outside (a climbing snake might conceivably gain a bellyhold

Never handle a dead rattlesnake. Lingering reflexes may cause it to be dangerous for an hour or more. (Some "old wives' tales" are true!)

in the curve), keep the outside of the wall free of vegetation, and make sure there's no "crawl space" under the gate.

A wall is probably a good idea if you're rearing small children in rattlesnake country. You don't need to enclose your whole yard; just create

a "safe zone" where the children can play outdoors. You can inspect the area periodically to keep it free of other hazards, too.

Side benefits: the wall will also (1) help keep the kids from wandering off to parts unknown, (2) keep desert animals from drowning in your swimming pool, and (3) protect your prize plants from hungry rabbits and javelina.

♦ *Are there any alternatives?*

If you don't have small children, and you're not too afraid of snakes yourself, a wall probably isn't necessary—a little

vigilance may be all that's required. Find out what snakes live in your neighborhood and how to tell the dangerous from the harmless ones. It will be interesting to learn more about the creatures. Family members should also learn to take care where they put their hands and feet and to use a flashlight outdoors at night. These are habits that will serve everyone well in the greater desert outdoors.

A "GILA MONSTER" IN EVERY GARAGE

People in the Sonoran Desert are frequently startled to find small, yellowish or pinkish, darkly blotched or banded lizards hiding under debris in their garages or yards. Baby Gila monsters?

Usually not; much more often they're western banded geckos (*Coleonyx variegatus*), but it's not surprising people misidentify these creatures. Their color patterns are superficially Gila-monster-like, and both lizards have thick tails (carrying stored fat reserves). Here's how to tell them apart.

Size. Even the largest adult banded gecko is less than six inches from the snout to the tip of the tail. The average *hatchling* Gila monster is longer than that, and much more thick-bodied. It can eventually grow to a length of more than twenty inches!

Skin. A Gila monster's skin has large beadlike scales, but the skin of a banded gecko is delicate and soft, and you might need a magnifier to see the scales.

Snout. All black on a Gila monster, but mottled on a banded gecko.

Eyes. Rounded pupils in Gila monsters, vertical pupils in banded geckos—but if you're not sure which you're looking at, do you really want to get close enough to see this?

The differences in the eyes reflect the animals' activity patterns: Gila monsters are **diurnal** (day active) but banded geckos are **nocturnal**, so we usually find them hiding under objects during the day. The gecko in your garage patrols the premises after dark, hunting insects, spiders and other small **arthropods**. It's absolutely harmless to you and performs its extermination services *gratis*.

Banded geckos are fragile creatures, so if you want a closer look try gently coaxing it into a box or jar rather than catching it by hand. It may raise its head and tail belligerently and—surprisingly—squeak. Don't worry. Its bark is definitely worse than its bite!

Western banded gecko

Even without a wall you can reduce the likelihood that rattlesnakes will show up by keeping your yard free of clutter. (This may also prevent problems with certain insects and their relatives. See Questions 22 and 23.) You don't need to remove the native vegetation, but if you're very concerned you might consider clearing small strips next to walkways.

It also helps to leave the harmless snakes alone. They may take the same prey as the rattlesnakes, and keeping prey numbers down will make your yard less tempting to the rattlers.

◆ What should I do if I find a rattlesnake in my yard?

Many people make special efforts to bring desert wildlife to their yards. Rattlesnakes are wildlife, too. One thing you can do when one turns up is enjoy it—from a safe distance, of course! Eventually it will go away.

If the snake worries you, or if you're concerned it may return at an inopportune moment, you can have an experienced person remove it to a distant place. Local fire departments will often perform the service, as will some pest control companies. Your state game and fish department may be able to advise you.

The worst thing you could do is try to kill the snake. Rattlesnakes have a role to play in the desert world. Besides, you could easily get hurt.

◆ What happens to relocated rattlesnakes?

Rattlesnakes are usually relocated for our benefit, not theirs, so few studies have been done to find out how the snakes fare.

For many years the Desert Museum has been marking and moving rattlesnakes found on the grounds. Sometimes they come back. Many released a mile away have returned, and one found its way home from 2½ miles away!

As for survival, the limited information available suggests that some relocated snakes don't make it in their new surroundings, while others do fine. Much probably depends on where they're released. A snake from the cactus-covered foothills probably won't do well in a valley-bottom creosote flat.

The most effective and humane way to relocate rattlesnakes seems to be to release them at least a mile away in habitat similar to where they were found—but not in someone else's back yard!

Related questions:

Q16. How can I keep wild animals from eating the plants in my garden?
Q22. How can I keep dangerous scorpions and spiders out of my house?
Q23. How can I tell if the bees in my yard are Africanized?
Q25. What kind of snake is in my yard?
Q37. How can I avoid dangerous encounters with rattlers and Gila monsters?
Q38. Are there other venomous reptiles in the Sonoran Desert?

How can I stop woodpeckers from making holes in my house?

ANSWER: *Persistence.*

If you're setting out to solve a woodpecker problem, you're about to match wits with a very determined adversary. Woodpeckers are powerfully motivated to peck wood. In nature this characteristic behavior provides them with both food (insects) and nesting sites. Unfortunately for us, wooden siding, beams, and posts (and sometimes stucco) encourage woodpeckers to do what comes naturally. Discouraging them often requires considerable ingenuity.

Here are some of the many remedies others have tried. Sometimes they work.

• Scare the bird with bright objects that move in the breeze: metal pie pans or can lids hung on strings, long colorful streamers or strips of aluminum foil, toy plastic twirlers, or wind socks—especially ones with a metallic sheen.

• Scare the bird with a fake owl or snake.

Sadly, this often works only for a day or two.

• Scare the bird by running outside, shouting, and clapping your hands. Good for five minutes of relief.

• Cover the hole where the bird has been working. Use a metal patch, but be sure not to wall off an active nest. Of course, the bird may just begin again a few inches away. But it may not.

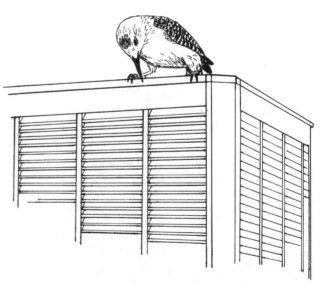

• Cover the entire area with something impenetrable: half-inch chicken wire hung an inch away from the wood, or metal flashing nailed directly over the surface. Ugly, but usually effective.

• Treat the area with something unpleasant: linseed oil or wood

---

ON KEEPING ONE'S PERSPECTIVE

Perhaps the best advice that can be given to someone with a woodpecker situation is not to take it too seriously. Think of it as a game with a worthy opponent, not a battle with a malevolent enemy. It's a game you can win if you play intelligently, keep at it, and don't concede in exasperation.

If attitude adjustments fail and you're tempted to end the contest by shooting your opponent, think again. Not only would you be endangering your neighbors, breaking the law, and killing an interesting desert creature, but another woodpecker would probably move right in to take its place. Then you'd be starting the whole game over again—and with a fresh opponent!

---

preservative. A bad-tasting concoction like "Ropel" (available at nurseries) may work if applied directly to a hole in the making.

No two houses or birds are alike. It will probably take some experimentation to find the tactic, or combination of tactics, that works at *your* home with *your* woodpecker. The sooner you get started the better. A bird that's made a habit of

---

drilling into your house is harder to deal with than one that's taking its first few tentative pecks.

Be creative! If you come up with something original and effective, call the Desert Museum so the staff can share it with other beleaguered homeowners. You are not alone.

• *Why does the woodpecker pound on my metal evaporative cooler?*

Probably not to find food or make a nest. Woodpeckers have unmusical voices and use rhythmic pounding the way many other birds use song: to declare their territories and attract mates. They're more apt to do it during the breeding season. Woodpeckers choose the noisiest objects to pound on because these broadcast the strongest message to other woodpeckers— not because it's most annoying to us!

Some of the "scare tactics" listed above may discourage these winged percussionists. It also works to mute their instruments by covering them with something soft, such as thick cloth.

Related questions:

Q16. How can I keep wild animals from eating the plants in my garden?
Q28. Why do packrats keep making houses in my car's engine compartment?

QUESTION

Why do packrats keep making houses in my car's engine compartment?

ANSWER: *Because it's such an inviting place to live.*

Packrats in the Sonoran Desert often build their houses under trees and prickly pears, but they also frequently make dens in protected rock niches and caves. To a packrat your engine compartment is just another cave. Because the animal's ancestors evolved in the absence of automobiles, it has no idea that this particular cave may someday make a loud noise and move.

Unfortunately, the packrat doesn't just drag in sticks and cholla joints; it also chews on the wires and hoses. This isn't a calculated effort to immobilize your vehicle—though it certainly can have this effect! The packrat is probably just rearranging its living quarters, or satisfying a rodent's primal urge to gnaw.

✦ *What can I do about it?*

Buy or borrow a humane live trap. (Call an animal feed store or your state game and fish department to find one.) Bait the trap with peanut butter on a cracker and put it near the car at night. The next day transport the packrat to some more appropriate habitat, where there are rocks and prickly pears, but no automobiles.

Of course, if you do nothing else another packrat is likely to move into the vacated compartment. If you can put the car in an enclosed garage, that should prevent a reinfestation. If the car is already in a garage, then packrats must have a way to get in. Find the entrance and seal it off securely with wood, heavy screening, sheet metal, or cement.

If your vehicle must be kept outdoors the problem is more difficult—especially if the car is infrequently driven. Smelly repellents seldom work, and the odors inevitably get into the passenger compartment. (Mothballs are among the worst this way. Don't even think about it.) Simple suggestion: try leaving the hood partly open. If that doesn't work, repeated trapping may be your best bet.

Declaring war on the neighborhood rodents is never the answer; there will always be legions of replacements for the fallen. And don't use poisons. They'd harm other animals—possibly including you.

✦ *What about the packrat in my attic?*

The solution is the same as for the one in your car: trap and relocate the animal, then seal off the entryways. Just in case you have a packrat family (a mother and young), repeat the procedure until you're sure you've gotten them all. Repellents really aren't necessary, and some of those often recommended (loud music, bright lights, ammonia) might irritate you as much as the rodents.

Once you have the house sealed off, check for chewed electrical wiring. There's

PACKRATS AND PALEOECOLOGISTS

Packrats (*Neotoma* species), called "woodrats" in most field guides, are attractive rodents about the size of house rats, but with fur-covered tails and light-colored feet. They're **nocturnal** and secretive, so you're much more likely to see their debris-pile homes than the builders themselves. These messy-looking dwellings are actually elaborate structures, with multiple entrances and passageways, and they shield their occupants well from both predators and the weather.

In dry caves packrat refuse piles (middens), cemented together by evaporated urine, can last tens of thousands of years. **Paleoecologists** identify species of plants from fragments and seeds in these deposits, judge their age by **radiocarbon dating**, and reconstruct how plant communities have changed over time. Thanks to packrats we know that during the last Ice Age, which ended about 11,000 years ago, much of what is now the desert Southwest was home to pinyon pines, junipers, and oaks! Desert plants began to move in from warmer refuges as the climate heated up, and today's Sonoran Desert **communities** took shape only about four or five thousand years ago.

It had happened many times before. In the last two million years the desert has retreated fifteen to twenty times during as many Ice Ages, and re-advanced in the warm intervals between. We seem to live in one of the warm "interglacials" now. The oaks may return—and more than once!

Packrat nest

no need to worry about the packrats still living outdoors. They're interesting native wildlife. (See sidebar, previous page.)

♦ Aren't insects that live with the packrats also a problem?

Conenose bugs (*Triatoma* species), known also as "kissing bugs" or "Hualapai tigers," are common parasites in packrat houses, where they suck the blood of their rodent hosts. When they get into our houses they bite us, too. There are several species in the Sonoran Desert, all ½ to 1 inch long, black or brown with orangeish marks along the sides of the abdomen, and odd, tiny, conical heads.

Conenose bug

Most people are bitten at night, and thanks to a numbing saliva injected by the insect, they aren't aware it's happening. Unfortunately, some people become sensitized to the saliva, and the results can be life-threatening. For symptoms and treatments, see Appendix C.

Conenose bugs most often get inside houses when they're flying about on spring or summer nights. At these times they're irresistibly drawn to bright lights outside houses, and as night ends they seek indoor hiding places. It's obvious what to do: turn off outdoor lights at night and seal or screen potential entryways. The latter strategy is also effective against dangerous **arachnids** (Question 22) and Africanized bees (Question 23).

Once your house is sealed up, nearby packrat houses shouldn't be a problem, though you might want to relocate a packrat whose house is built right up against yours. To find the bugs that are already indoors, search dark places, especially in bedding, under furniture, and in closets. Don't poison your own habitat with insecticides.

♦ Should I be concerned about hantavirus?

No one is known to have been infected with **hantavirus** by contact with packrats or their leavings. However, packrats are known sometimes to carry the virus, so it's prudent to be cautious when trapping and moving packrats, and especially when cleaning up packrat houses after evicting the occupants. For more about hantavirus, including recommended clean-up procedures, see Appendix D.

Related questions:

Q22. How can I keep dangerous scorpions and spiders out of my house?
Q23. How can I tell if the bees in my yard are Africanized?
See also Appendix D: Hantavirus.

QUESTION

29

How can I protect my pets from coyotes and bobcats?

ANSWER: *By keeping your pets out of harm's way, and not attracting these two predators to your property.*

Coyotes are anything but finicky eaters. In natural desert habitats they feast on everything from crickets and cactus fruits to quail, cottontails, carrion, and deer. It's no stretch for them to add domestic cats and small dogs to their nutritional repertoire. Bobcats, on the other hand, have more refined tastes: they eat mostly rodents, rabbits, and jackrabbits (less often birds and lizards). They're less inclined to make a meal of your pet—but it happens!

Fortunately, there are things you can do to keep your dog or cat off the menu.

• Don't give your pet free run of the neighborhood. Stay with it when it's outdoors, and carry it or keep it on a leash when you take it for a walk. (There are other good reasons for controlling your pet—see sidebar, next page.)

• If you want to leave a small dog unattended in your yard, an enclosure will at least make it less convenient prey. A six-foot chain link fence with the base buried six inches in the soil is a good deterrent, but a highly motivated bobcat can jump over it. A solid wall keeps your pet out of sight,

but it's easier for a coyote or bobcat to jump up on top. Still, any barrier is better than none.

• If you provide food and water for birds and rabbits, the food, water, birds, and rabbits may attract coyotes and bobcats. Avoid overdoing your wildlife feeding and watering. (See Question 17.) Spilled bird-seed from feeders often attracts coyotes.

• Avoid providing other temptations around your home. Don't leave pet food outdoors, and keep garbage containers securely covered.

• If you see a coyote or bobcat near your house you can make the neighborhood seem less hospitable by shouting and

clapping your hands, though it's best to avoid up-close confrontations. (But if you don't have outdoor pets and the animal's not making a nuisance of itself, why not just reach for your binoculars?)

PREDATORY PETS

Free-running cats and dogs aren't just prey for coyotes and bobcats; they're predators themselves. Unleashed dogs taken on hikes may leave the trail and frighten and harass desert wildlife. **Feral** dogs sometimes form packs that chase down and kill livestock and native animals.

Free-ranging cats may be an even more serious problem. Cats are believed to kill several billion birds yearly in the United States and an even larger number of small mammals. Feral cats aren't the only culprits; well-fed pets also indulge their instinctual urge to hunt. Little is yet known about the impact of these feline predators on desert ecosystems, but pet cats regularly kill small desert mammals like pocket mice, as well as many lizards and birds.

Neither coyotes nor bobcats confine their activities to the open desert and the suburbs. Coyotes are quite common in urban habitats, and even bobcats show up surprisingly often in cities, especially where cottontails graze on watered lawns.

◆ Are these animals a threat to me or my children?

Not ordinarily, if you leave them alone.

Like most other wild animals, coyotes and bobcats have a natural wariness around human beings, so they tend to keep their distance. But coyotes, especially, can become habituated to people. Deliberately or inadvertently feeding a coyote can replace its fear of people with the expectation of a reward, setting the stage for an unpleasant encounter. Attempts at hand feeding lie behind most bites by coyotes (and other wild animals). If you're tempted to feed a coyote anyway, remember: it doesn't need the food, and you may turn it into a nuisance animal with a very reduced life expectancy.

The possibility of either a coyote or a bobcat taking a very small child is extremely remote, but there are many other reasons not to leave infants and toddlers unattended outdoors—and not just in the desert.

Children old enough to understand should be taught that coyotes and bobcats are wild animals, not pets like dogs or house cats. If they come across one of these interesting creatures outdoors, they should watch from a distance until it leaves, or walk (not run) away themselves, but not approach it. They should never try to play with it or feed it.

This is good advice for grown-ups as well. Seeing a coyote in the wild is nothing to fear—you'll probably find it trots off before you've had enough time to enjoy it. Seeing a wild bobcat is a rare and wonderful occasion. May you and your children be so fortunate!

Related questions:

Q16. How can I keep wild animals from eating the plants in my garden?
Q17. How can I attract desert wildlife to my yard?
Q26. How can I keep rattlesnakes out of my yard?

Section 3

Enjoying the Outdoors

I T'S TIME TO REVEAL a well-kept secret: the deadly desert is a myth perpetrated by desert residents themselves. How better to impress the relatives in Ohio than with tales of searing heat, poisonous cactus spines, and malevolent rattlesnakes? Only the bravest souls would venture outdoors in such a place!

The fact is, it's safe out there—not perfectly safe, but what place is? Every place has its hazards; there are rattlesnakes in Oregon, too, and summer in the Sonoran Desert is no more dangerous than winter in the Midwest.

These last few questions will help you be prepared for the desert outdoors, so you can enjoy it worry-free. (But don't tell your friends back East!)

QUESTION

What might I bring on a hike to help me enjoy the desert?

ANSWER: *As little as possible.*

Part of the fun of venturing into any wild place is the feeling of being unencumbered, so the trick is never to take too much. Here are a few items that are especially likely to add to your enjoyment without weighing you down.

• *Magnifying glass.* The desert is intriguing on every scale, from the grandest landscape to the least conspicuous **belly flower**. Even an inexpensive magnifier can bring you eye-to-eye with a beetle—and help you pull out tiny cactus spines as well!

• *Binoculars.* Choose carefully, and be sure to try them out before buying. The fact that a friend raves about his binoculars doesn't mean they'll work well with *your* eyes. Consider one of the miniature pairs—in twilight the image may be dimmer than in full-size instruments, but you won't end the day with a sore neck.

• *Camera.* You don't need to be Ansel Adams to get pleasure from picture taking, nor do you need to carry his equipment. (Sometimes he used a mule!) If you're a novice, start with something inexpensive, lightweight, and simple—don't be seduced by bells and whistles. And don't forget film and a spare battery.

• *Notebook.* Field notes are a good device to help you look more closely at

Excessive heat can shift the colors of photographic film and addle the electronic brains of modern automatic cameras. Bury your extra film deep in your day bag, and keep your camera out of the sun as much as you can.

your surroundings, and a wonderful way to evoke the experience of a special hike many years later. (See Question 42.)

• *Field guides.* No one wants a library on his back, so why not pick a focus for the day—say, wildflowers or lizards? If you come across something to look up in one of the guides you left at home,

> *Water isn't all we lose when we perspire. To make up for your salt loss, carry a salty snack like crackers or pretzels to nibble, or have something salty in your lunch. This helps prevent heat cramps.*

you can always take its picture or sketch it in your notebook for later identification. Some suggested titles are listed in the bibliography.

Many people assemble a simple desert hiking kit in a day bag and keep it always ready to go. You'll want to include a few comfort and safety items, too. Read on.

• *What else should I put in my pack?*

You won't need much. These are some suggestions for useful, lightweight items.

• *Map.* United States Geological Survey (USGS) topographic maps are excellent. They can be purchased at some outdoor equipment stores, or photocopied at libraries. Some people like to carry a compass, too.

• *Small flashlight with fresh batteries.* Good for emergencies and essential for walking after dark in rattlesnake season.

• *Small first aid kit.* Tweezers, bandages, a magnifying glass, and aspirin.

• *Comb.* For removing cholla joints. (See Question 33.)

• *Lip salve.*

• *Pocket knife.*

There are a few other emergency items you might consider:

• *Snake venom extractor.* This isn't the old-fashioned "cut and suck" kit. See Appendix C.

• *Waterproof matches.*

• *Whistle.* For emergencies.

• *Signaling mirror.* Has a hole to help direct the reflected beam. Also useful when removing cactus spines from inconvenient parts of your anatomy.

Of course, the most important things you'll need to have with you on a hike are water and proper clothing. More on that in Question 31.

Related questions:

Q31. What precautions should I take when hiking in the desert?
Q33. Are cactus spines poisonous?
Q34. Why don't I see very many animals when I hike in the desert?
Q42. What else can I do to explore the desert?
See also Appendix C: Venomous Bites and Stings.

QUESTION

What precautions should I take when hiking in the desert?

ANSWER: *Safe desert hiking is mostly a matter of common sense, carrying enough water, and dressing appropriately.*

Except for the climate, hiking in the desert isn't that different from hiking anywhere else, and most of the same rules apply. Here are a few tips for playing it safe in cactus land.

• Let someone know where you're going and when you expect to return.

• When you can, hike with a companion.

• Don't overdo it. If you're a novice hiker or a newcomer to the desert, stick to short outings until you've become acclimated.

• Even if you're experienced, avoid hiking in the middle of a hot day. Even lizards have enough sense to spend that time under a rock. Take a siesta.

• Don't forget you're among cacti. *Never* back up without looking first.

• Be alert for interesting encounters with snakes. (For more on that subject, see Question 37.)

FLASH!...BOOM!

Lightning is among the Sonoran Desert's most dramatic entertainments, but enjoyment from a distance is infinitely preferable to audience participation. What should you do if you're unexpectedly caught outdoors in an electrical storm?

If you can, take refuge inside your car. In a direct lightning strike electricity will usually pass over the surface of a hard top automobile (not a convertible) and leave the occupants unscathed—but startled out of their wits! So to avoid an accident caused by your own jumpy nervous system, wait until the lightning stops before you drive away.

(Despite what you may have heard, it isn't the tires that provide protection. A few inches of insulating rubber won't impede a bolt of electricity that can jump through thousands of feet of air! What keeps you safe is the natural tendency of electricity to stay on the outsides of metal objects.

If you're not near a car, the key is to make yourself "electrically inconspicuous"— as unlikely as possible to be singled out for a strike. If you're in a very open area seek a low spot (but not a wash—beware of flash flooding) and crouch down with your hands on your knees. You're somewhat safer in a fairly well-vegetated desert area because the lightning has more "choices" where to strike. But don't stand under an especially tall tree and of course not right next to a large saguaro!

A camping tent may make you feel secure, but it may be unsafe, especially if it's set up in an open area or has a metal center pole.

If you're caught on a high ridge or mountaintop, you're in a truly dangerous situation. Avoid any prominent outcrops. If the storm is approaching, your best bet may be to retreat quickly downhill. If the storm has already arrived, all you can do is crouch down—in a sheltered niche if possible—and ponder how to avoid a similar situation next time.

And that's your best lightning safety strategy: don't let yourself get caught outdoors in an electrical storm! If you remember that they usually happen in the afternoons and evenings during the summer monsoon (see Question 2 and Question 3), you can avoid an unduly electrifying experience.

• Most important, carry enough water and dress sensibly (see below).

◆ How much water should I bring?

More than you think you'll need. Perspiration is how your body cools itself, and you'll have to replace every drop you perspire. The amount depends on the weather, the length and difficulty of the hike, and your body's special characteristics.

You'll learn how much water to carry as you gain experience. Meanwhile, bear in mind that an adult walking at 100°F may perspire a quart or more per hour. You'd probably rather nap under a mesquite when it's that hot, but these numbers suggest that a single quart canteen may not be enough for even a short hike in very warm weather, and a gallon may not be too much for a full day out—even with a mid-day siesta.

And don't just carry the water; drink it! Our bodies often don't tell us when we need water, so sip periodically even if you aren't thirsty. If you *do* feel thirsty, you're

> *Even if you're shaded from the direct sun you can receive a serious dose of ultraviolet radiation from the clear blue sky. It's also quite possible to get a sunburn on a cloudy day.*

already becoming dehydrated. Be especially sure to drink plenty at mealtime.

Always keep an eye on your water supply. It's much better to turn back than to run out.

◆ What clothing is best for desert hiking?

Protection from skin-damaging **ultraviolet** light is one of the chief concerns in choosing desert attire. A hat is always advisable, especially a broad-brimmed model that shades your entire head and neck from the sun and sky. UV protective sunglasses are good for your eyes.

Some desert hikers prefer to wear short-sleeved shirts and short pants, and to protect their arms and legs with sunscreen. Others prefer long sleeves and long pants. Which you choose is a matter of personal preference, but there are clear advantages to covering your skin with cloth. Sunlight on the skin can be very uncomfortable in hot weather, and loose,

NO SWEAT?

On a hot day with low humidity your skin may be so dry that you think you're not perspiring. Don't be fooled into believing you don't need water. Your perspiration is simply evaporating immediately on contact with the air. To prove it, try wrapping your hand in plastic for a few minutes.

Longtime desert dwellers are often convinced they've "learned" to sweat less, but there's no way around the physics of evaporative cooling. In fact, as people acclimate to desert heat they increase their ability to perspire. They sweat more, not less.

benefit: Africanized bees are more likely to attack dark objects, which seem to resemble the animals that prey on honeybee colonies in Africa. So even light-colored hats and day bags are a good idea. (If you come across a honey bee colony on your hike, keep your distance.)

As for footwear, sturdy boots still give the best support and the best protection from cactus spines and rattlesnakes.

Finally, don't forget that the desert isn't always hot and dry. Carry rain gear during the rainy seasons, and be sure to bring a jacket or windbreaker for cool evenings, windy winter days, or higher elevations.

Related questions:

Great horned owl

breathable clothing actually reduces the amount of water lost in perspiration. Long sleeves and pants also protect against scratchy vegetation, irritating insects, and (to a lesser degree) rattlesnakes.

Light-colored clothing is cooler because it absorbs less sunlight. A side

QUESTION

If I run out of water in the desert can I get some from a barrel cactus?

ANSWER: *Perhaps, but it would be truly a desperation measure.*

Yes, some Sonoran Desert Indians have extracted moisture from barrel cacti, and yes, others have occasionally done it, too, but there are compelling reasons not to try to replicate this legendary feat yourself.

1. It's hard to get inside a barrel cactus. Many desert animals would be pleased to plunder that hidden moisture hoard, so it's no accident a barrel cactus is extraordinarily well fortified. Its largest spines are stout, curved, and easily hook your flesh, and its skin is extremely tough.

2. There's no tempting pool of clear water inside a barrel cactus, only plant

While the stems, joints, and pads of most cacti are toxic to some degree, no cactus fruits are poisonous. In fact, some—saguaro and prickly pear fruits, for example—are temptingly tasty. Why the difference? It only harms a cactus when something munches on its growing parts, but it helps when an animal devours a fruit, carries off the seeds in its gut, and plants them elsewhere— with a dose of fertilizer!

tissue resembling a damp, slimy sponge. Moisture must be laboriously pounded, squeezed, or chewed out of this stuff, and by some accounts it doesn't taste very good.

3. At hot, dry times of year a barrel cactus may have limited moisture reserves, so you may not gain much for all your efforts. You might even sweat away as much moisture trying to break into the plant as you would gain if you succeeded.

TEETOTALERS

Not surprisingly, many desert mammals are physiologically better qualified than we are for life in a dry land. Among the most remarkable is the kangaroo rat, the famous "rat that never drinks," yet subsists entirely on a diet of dry desert seeds. How does it do it?

It manufactures its own water. This may sound miraculous, but all animals—including you—produce water as an inevitable by-product of burning their food. A kangaroo rat is no better at creating this **oxidation water** than any other animal. It can live without drinking not because it's unusually good at making water, but because it's unusually good at holding onto the water it makes.

A kangaroo rat doesn't perspire. It lacks sweat glands, and it doesn't need them because it leaves its underground burrow only in the cool of the night. The humidity inside its burrow reduces other kinds of evaporation from its body, and its labyrinthine nasal passages trap moisture it might otherwise exhale. It produces very dry feces and, thanks to extraordinarily efficient kidneys, highly concentrated urine and very little of it.

A kangaroo rat might dry out anyway if subtleties in its diet didn't tweak its water budget just enough to keep it in balance. The "dry" desert seeds the animal gathers actually contain small but useful quantities of moisture absorbed from the night air, and any stored seeds stay moist in the burrow. Even the precise menu matters: high-carbohydrate seeds rather than seeds rich in fats or proteins. Burning fats would create excessive heat and the need for evaporative cooling, and the waste products from extra proteins would increase urine flow.

"K-rats" are such perfect examples of desert adaptation that it's perhaps not surprising nature has arrived at similar designs more than once—a wonderful example of **convergent evolution**. There are small jumping rodents very much like kangaroo rats in Old World deserts, including the jerboas and gerbils of Africa and Asia and certain hopping mice in Australia. And in case you're wondering, there are such things as "rat kangaroos" Down Under—but they're something completely different!

4. Only one species of barrel cactus is known to yield potable moisture: the fishhook barrel (*Ferocactus wislizeni*). Many other cacti (including other barrels) are toxic, so if you couldn't recognize the right plant with certainty, you'd be in danger of poisoning yourself. The toxins probably wouldn't kill you, but the likely effects—vomiting and diarrhea—are among the worst possible for anyone already suffering from dehydration.

5. All cacti are protected by law in both Arizona and California.

• Are there better ways to get water in the desert?

People have suggested many stratagems for obtaining emergency water in the desert—among them following animal trails to water holes, digging in washes and dry streambeds, and improvising solar stills. Many books (including some of those listed in the bibliography) describe such methods in detail. But by far the easiest, safest, and most reliable way to get water in the desert is from a faucet before you leave home.

Take more than enough water with you (see Question 31), travel with a companion—in two vehicles if you're driving in some out of the way place—and it's highly unlikely you'll ever have need for such "desert survival skills."

Related questions:

Q5. How can I tell cacti from other spiny desert plants?
Q31. What precautions should I take when hiking in the desert?
Q33. Are cactus spines poisonous?
Q40. What precautions should I take when driving in the desert?

Gambel's quail

Are cactus spines poisonous?

ANSWER: *No, this is just a myth.*

Getting stuck by cactus spines isn't one of life's more pleasant experiences, but when it happens to you—and if you spend time outdoors in the desert, sooner or later, inevitably, it will—at least being poisoned is something you won't need to worry about.

Still, try to remove spines right away, and not just because they hurt. Left in the skin they're more likely to cause local inflammation as your immune system reacts both to the spines themselves and to any bacteria residing on their surface.

As with all deep puncture wounds, tetanus infection is a remote but real possibility. Cacti are an extra reason for desert dwellers to keep their booster shots up to date.

◆ **What's the best way to remove cactus spines?**

An elaborate folk technology has evolved to deal with this problem in all its variations. Incidentally, there are wild cacti in all the contiguous states except Maine, New Hampshire, and Vermont, so desert dwellers don't enjoy a monopoly in these mild forms of torture.

• Large spines that haven't penetrated very far can usually be pulled out with the fingers, but deeply embedded spines may need to be extracted with a pair of pliers.

> *Jumping cholla joints don't jump; they just seem to. When you're surprised by one fastened to your leg, it's easy to imagine it leaped onto you when you weren't looking.*

• The jumping cholla and its invitingly named cousin, the teddy bear cholla, present a special hazard. If you carelessly brush against one of these, an entire stem segment—a joint—may detach itself from the plant and attach itself painfully to you. Your immediate impulse may be to reach for it with your bare hand. That is the worst thing you could possibly do.

Instead, try improvising a pair of tongs from rocks or sticks. Better yet, insert the teeth of a comb between yourself and the joint, and flip the offending object off your body. But before you do this, make sure no one is standing near the anticipated trajectory! More than one person has transferred a cholla joint to a companion in just this way.

If the joint is very firmly attached, you may need to cut the spines with strong scissors or wire cutters and get out the pliers.

• In addition to their more conventional spines, prickly pears brandish clusters of fragile, hairlike, barbed needles called **glochids.** (Chollas have glochids, too, but they cause fewer problems.) Glochids are

WHAT GOOD ARE CACTUS SPINES?

Cactus spines didn't evolve to punish clumsy hikers. Their chief function, as one might expect, is to protect cacti from hungry animals. It doesn't always work. Javelina devour entire prickly pear pads, spines and all, and thirsty jackrabbits and cottontails nibble carefully between the **areoles.** Spines may offer little impediment to cactus-consuming bugs and beetles, though flying insects occasionally blunder into them, impaling themselves helplessly on the tips.

Spines of some of the more densely-cloaked cacti collectively shade the plants from overheating and sunburn, and the thick mat of spines at the growing tip of a saguaro or barrel cactus provides insulation against freezing on clear winter nights. A cholla segment that affixes itself by means of its spines to a passing deer or hiker serves a reproductive purpose: it may eventually sprout roots after being disengaged some distance away. (See Question 7 sidebar, page 24.)

Animals sometimes turn cactus spines to their own advantage. Packrats pile the fiercely spined joints of chollas around their dens, discouraging predators. Certain birds seem to nest in spiny chollas for similar reasons, but must protect their own nestlings from the hazard. Cactus wren nestlings are safe inside covered nests, while curve-billed thrasher parents systematically break off the tips of spines near their nest cups. Mummified snakes are sometimes found entangled in cholla spines— the aftermath of failed nest raids.

Even human beings have found uses for cactus spines. Native people have fashioned sewing needles from them and used curved barrel cactus spines as fish hooks. A stout prickly pear spine (with the tip snapped off) makes a fine toothpick, and cactus spines were once sold as record playing needles for wind-up Victrolas!

Hedgehog cactus

Teddy bear cholla

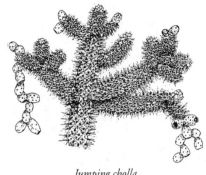

Jumping cholla

devilishly sharp. What's worse, being punctured by a single one is an uncommon event; usually they're delivered *en masse*.

Fingers are poor tools for removing glochids; they tend to break off the spines or get stuck themselves. Tweezers work, but it requires considerable delicacy and patience, and perhaps a magnifying glass, to remove several dozen of the things. An interesting approach to the multiple glochid problem is to coat the affected area with white glue, allow it to dry, then peel it off.

The truly nasty thing about glochids is their tendency to break off just above skin level, beyond the reach of tweezers or glue, but perfectly configured to issue pointed reminders of their presence whenever anything brushes your skin. You can try to dig the spines out with a needle—if you can find them—or resign yourself to living with them. Take heart: eventually they'll dissolve or be expelled.

Related questions:

Q5. How can I tell cacti from other spiny desert plants?
Q30. What might I bring on a hike to help me enjoy the desert?
Q31. What precautions should I take when hiking in the desert?
Q32. If I run out of water in the desert can I get some from a barrel cactus?

QUESTION

Why don't I see very many animals when I hike in the desert?

ANSWER: *Perhaps because you and the animals are on different schedules.*

Many of us desert humans follow a nine-to-five routine, a way of life that would be utterly impractical if it weren't for air conditioners and evaporative coolers.

> *Mad dogs and Englishmen go out in the midday sun.*
>
> — NOEL COWARD

Other desert animals aren't constrained by our peculiar customs; they follow the dictates of the climate. If we want to meet them in their natural habitats we need to set our schedules by their biological clocks.

Most desert birds have two main activity periods: a major peak in early morning and a minor one in the evening. Birds are taking it easy—and therefore harder to find—precisely when people are habitually most active. To see the most desert birds you need to be outdoors and looking when the sun comes up. Better yet, catch the "dawn chorus" of awakening birds as the sky lightens *before* sunrise. It's well worth the effort.

Many desert mammals beat the heat by being **nocturnal** or **crepuscular** (active in the twilight at either end of the day). Some, like javelina, adjust their schedules to the seasons, becoming more **diurnal** (day active) when the weather is cool. Just as with birds, evening and early morning

are almost always good times to see desert mammals, but midday almost never is.

For an especially rewarding desert wildlife experience, try a walk after dark on a warm summer night. (See sidebar, this page.)

♦ Are some desert places better than others for seeing wildlife?

Yes: places with water.

Perennial streams and rivers are the Sonoran Desert's prime wildlife "hot spots." Not only does a stream offer drinking water—a precious commodity in itself—but the dense **riparian** vegetation also provides unusually abundant food, hiding places, and nesting sites. These rare habitats deserve our special care. Do your best not to disturb nesting birds, and avoid trampling the lush vegetation.

Even a dry **wash** or **arroyo** is a focal point for desert wildlife. There's usually no water at the surface, but it may flow beneath the sand and gravel, if only briefly during a rainstorm. This is enough to make the vegetation along even a small drainageway thicker than elsewhere, significantly enhancing the habitat for many kinds of animals.

A sandy wash is a convenient highway for desert creatures and the human beings who like to look for them. But stay out of washes and arroyos in a rainstorm, even if the rain is falling far upstream. Flash floods are a genuine hazard in the desert,

DESERT NIGHT LIFE

Creatures of daylight that we are, we may find it hard to grasp how dramatically the desert comes to life after dark. During the heat of the summer the activities of desert animals are the exact reverse of our everyday human experience: days are times of relative quiet and rest, while nights bustle with activity.

A desert walk on a summer night can be a revelation, especially after a monsoon rain. Rattlesnakes are part of the excitement, so always use a flashlight, and if possible stick to broad trails, roads, and washes. (See Question 37.) Try holding the flashlight next to your head, to better see the eyeshine of desert animals. Even better, invest in a headlamp, which will free your hands.

Every once in a while stop, turn off your light, and drink in the sensations of the desert night. Wildflowers will have opened in the moonlight, spreading their scent for nocturnal pollinators. Listen for the sounds of the "night shift"—the hoots of owls, the howls of coyotes—carried on the warm breeze. It's enough to make us daytime chauvinists regret the error of our ways.

*In a region characterized by dryness, it's not surprising that the banks of rivers and streams should be extraordinary places. The Sonoran Desert's **riparian** communities are focal points of biodiversity—and arguably its most significant wildlife habitats. Unfortunately, many such habitats have been degraded or lost in the last century and a half, largely due to the activities of humankind.*

and not only to people on foot. (See Question 40.)

Biologists sometimes study desert animals by watching isolated watering places such as natural stone tanks or **tinajas** in arid canyons, but they're very careful not to interfere with the animals when they are getting a drink. If you wish to try this, stay well hidden and at least several hundred feet from the water hole, as well as any approaches to it. If there's no suitable viewpoint, leave the area. Remember: drinking may be a life-and-death matter for these wild creatures. Seeing them do it isn't a life-and-death matter for you.

◆ *Is there anything else I can do to see more desert wildlife?*

Even if you're not staking out a water hole, it's often a good idea to take a break from hiking and sit quietly, waiting for animals to show themselves. Be patient. After a while some creatures may become accustomed to your presence and come out of hiding. Others may wander into the neighborhood without noticing you. And you may eventually become aware of a well-camouflaged animal nearby—something you would have missed in your eagerness to get from here to there.

Finally, it may help to expand your concept of "wildlife." If you include the lizards, snakes, insects, spiders, and other small creatures, you'll never take a desert hike without finding some fascinating wildlife to enjoy—no matter what the season, time of day, or place.

Related questions:

Q3. Are there seasons in the Sonoran Desert?
Q30. What might I bring on a hike to help me enjoy the desert?
Q31. What precautions should I take when hiking in the desert?
Q36. If I find a desert tortoise, would it be all right to take it home as a pet?
Q37. How can I avoid dangerous encounters with rattlers and Gila monsters?
Q41. How can I minimize my impact on the desert?
Q42. What else can I do to explore the desert?

QUESTION
35

How dangerous are Sonoran Desert toads?

ANSWER: *Sonoran Desert toads pose no serious danger to people who are reasonably careful.*

Sonoran Desert toads (*Bufo alvarius*), sometimes called Colorado River toads, are hard to miss. They're the bullfrogs of the toad world, growing up to 7½ inches long—much larger than any other toads in Arizona or California. Adults are brownish or olive, but younger individuals tend to be lighter colored with reddish blotches. Except for the tiniest toadlets, they all have distinctive white warts at the corners of the mouth.

Slow-moving and lacking in physical defenses, all toads depend to some degree on chemical weaponry for protection against predators. Poisons are produced by glands all over a toad's skin, but especially in two raised **parotoid glands** behind the eyes. The Sonoran Desert toad's secretions are especially toxic: these substances can disrupt nerve and muscle function in a mammal naive enough to get one of these creatures in its mouth.

Unless you do something careless or foolish (see sidebar, next page) a Sonoran Desert toad has no method—or reason—to get its toxins into you. If you pick one up be sure not to touch your eyes or nose, or to handle food, until you've washed your hands. Other desert frogs and toads are less potent, but you should wash after touching them, too.

Incidentally, the water in your swimming pool will still be quite safe after a Sonoran Desert toad has been in it, but for the sake of the toads—and other desert animals in danger of drowning— you might consider a low wall to keep them out. Such a wall can have other benefits, too. (See Question 26.)

• Should children be allowed to handle Sonoran Desert toads?

Very small children are likely to put their fingers in their mouth after handling a toad, and some might try to suck on the toad itself! Don't let very small children handle Sonoran Desert toads. Older children shouldn't handle the animals without supervision, and should of course be taught to wash their hands afterwards.

Some children are fascinated by toads, others may be frightened, but any encounter with a desert amphibian is an opportunity for learning. Help children understand that people need to be cautious about toads but not afraid of them, and that we should do these interesting creatures no harm.

• How can I protect my dog from Sonoran Desert toads?

Dogs can be poisoned by Sonoran Desert toads in two quite different ways.

First, if a dog mouths a Sonoran Desert toad it may get a powerful dose of toad juice. The dog may be temporarily paralyzed or even die. If your dog has tasted a toad, wash out its mouth thoroughly with copious amounts of water. Use a garden hose if you can, but be careful not to drown your pet. If your dog shows symptoms, get it to a

veterinarian. Watch for excessive salivation, pawing at the mouth, uneven walking, restlessness, or lethargy.

HOLY SMOKE!

Are people more intelligent than their pets? Given the well-known effects of Sonoran Desert toads on curious dogs, the very last thing you might expect anyone to do with one of these poisonous amphibians is lick it. But people occasionally do exactly that in the mistaken belief it will get them "high." It won't. It will make them sick and could possibly kill them.

On the other hand, curious humans have found that smoking the dried secretions of Sonoran Desert toads actually can cause hallucinations. But don't try it. The effect is powerful, unpredictable, and possibly dangerous. Toad poison includes several highly toxic ingredients, only one of which is hallucinogenic, and the recipe varies greatly from toad to toad. The Sonoran Desert offers many opportunities to expand your mind without using chemicals—and without abusing the native fauna.

The second way a dog can be poisoned is indirectly. Toads don't drink; they absorb water through their skin by sitting on wet soil or in a puddle. A dog's water dish is a tempting artificial puddle for a toad on a nocturnal foray. The problem occurs the next morning, when the amphibian is long gone, and your dog takes a drink. Call a vet if you suspect your dog has been drinking toad tea.

Some dogs are disinclined to investigate toads. Others learn their lesson from a single unpleasant encounter. You may be able to train your dog to leave Sonoran Desert toads alone by arranging a supervised meeting with one.

If education fails you can always keep your dog indoors or inside a walled yard at night during toad season. Fortunately for your pet, not many Sonoran Desert toads are out and about until the summer **monsoon**, although some are active as early as May.

Finally, you can avoid brewing a toxic beverage for your pet by bringing its water dish indoors at night, or elevating the dish beyond the reach of thirsty amphibians.

Related questions:

Q3. Are there seasons in the Sonoran Desert?
Q9. What are the frogs I hear at night during the summer rains?
Q26. How can I keep rattlesnakes out of my yard?

Collared lizard

QUESTION

If I find a desert tortoise, would it be all right to take it home as a pet?

ANSWER: *No, you shouldn't take any animal from the wild as a pet, especially one as uncommon as a desert tortoise.*

Besides, it would be illegal. Desert tortoises are protected by state laws everywhere they naturally occur in the United States—and in some areas by federal law as well. In fact, not only shouldn't you take a wild tortoise home, you shouldn't even pick one up. Here's why.

Unlike us, a desert tortoise can reabsorb moisture from its bladder; in effect, it carries a built-in canteen. If you pick up a wild tortoise, the frightened reptile is likely to dump its water supply—a minor nuisance for you, but a major problem for the tortoise, which in a severe drought

could die before the next rainstorm allows it to refill!

♦ *If it's illegal to collect wild tortoises, how can people have them as pets?*

Unfortunately, some people take home wild tortoises despite the law. But it's also possible to gain the privilege of caring for a tortoise legally.

In both Arizona and California you may keep a tortoise that's given (not sold) to you by an individual who possesses it legally himself. It could be an animal that was taken from the wild years ago, when that was still legal, or it could be a descendant of one that was.

Another legal way to acquire a tortoise is through an approved tortoise adoption program, which accepts tortoises people can no longer keep, cares for them, and finds them new homes. The Arizona-Sonora Desert Museum runs such a program, and there are others, too—call your state game and fish department to find the one nearest you. The department will

also be able to tell you the legal details of possession, which differ slightly between Arizona and California.

Caring for a tortoise can be a wonderful experience, but it requires dedication and a carefully prepared back yard. It's also not quite like having a pet. A tortoise doesn't show affection like a dog or a cat, and it shouldn't be frequently handled. You don't really own it, either—you're just its legal custodian. And that can be a very long-term responsibility. Tortoises may live fifty years or even a century; your tortoise might outlive you!

• Where should I release a tortoise I can no longer care for?

You shouldn't. You should find someone else who can keep it or you should give it to an adoption program. It's actually illegal to let a captive tortoise go, for several reasons.

• Released long-term captive tortoises often don't survive. When suddenly thrust into a strange environment they don't know where to find food or shelter. And sometimes all the available territory may already be occupied by other tortoises.

• There are genetic differences between tortoises living in different areas. A tortoise let go in the wrong place might introduce inappropriate characteristics into a wild population.

• Perhaps most important, a released captive might carry a disease to wild tortoises. More on that below.

• Are tortoises endangered?

No, they're not in immediate danger of extinction, but they have much

to contend with. Understanding the threats requires a quick lesson in tortoise **biogeography.**

There are two distinct **populations** of desert tortoises in the United States, separated by a natural barrier to interbreeding: the Colorado River. Tortoises in the two populations differ in genetic make-up, appearance, and habits.

Most tortoises in the Sonoran Desert belong to the population east of the river. They mostly reside on the rocky slopes and upper **bajadas** of desert mountain ranges. Tortoises in the population west of the Colorado mostly live in the Mohave Desert. They occupy the plains and valleys between mountain ranges. (For more about this population, see sidebar, next page.)

Here are some of the threats faced by tortoises in the Sonoran Desert, east of the Colorado:

• *Habitat loss* to cities, suburbs, mines, and other developments is reducing the areas where tortoises can live.

• *Habitat isolation* by valley developments may prevent occasional interbreeding between tortoises from different mountain ranges—something perhaps necessary for their genetic health. (Scientists differ about how often tortoises crossed the valleys in centuries past.) Canals and highways are among the barriers to tortoise movement, and they also sometimes cause tortoise deaths by drowning and automobile impact.

• *Old World grasses* invading the desert are not necessarily harmful in themselves, but by filling in the spaces between the native desert plants they encourage wildfires that kill tortoises caught in the open. Entire desert communities are being permanently changed by exotic grasses

A CASE OF THE SNIFFLES

Wild tortoises sometimes get runny noses, but it's a disease beyond the efficacy of chicken soup. Upper respiratory tract disease, or URTD, is potentially deadly to at least some desert tortoises. Caused by an odd bacterium called a **mycoplasma**, it has killed many tortoises in some areas, while leaving those in other areas unscathed.

The two populations of tortoises on either side of the Colorado River have been affected very differently by URTD. Many tortoises west and north of the river (mostly in the Mohave Desert) have died from the disease—one reason why that population has been federally listed as threatened. Tortoises east and south of the Colorado have been little harmed, though they show evidence of exposure to the mycoplasma. Why the difference?

Scientists are still piecing together the puzzle. The desert tortoise evolved in what is now Mexico, in dry tropical forest habitats with generous summer rainfall. Tortoises west of the Colorado River now live where there is little, if any, summer rain. (See Question 2.) The stress of prolonged warm season droughts, especially after unusually dry winters, may sometimes reduce their resistance to disease. These tortoises also tend to have relatively high natural population densities (tortoises per square mile) and to share burrows, increasing opportunities for disease transmission.

Tortoises east and south of the river benefit from a more favorable climate, lower population densities, and solitary living arrangements. Some researchers suspect they may also have genetic resistance to the mycoplasma.

There are still many uncertainties about URTD, and scientists are concerned that other serious tortoise diseases could reach the United States through the exotic pet trade—good reasons never to release a captive tortoise into the wild!

and the fires they bring. (For more about this, see Question 8.)

• *Habitat degradation* by livestock grazing may be a problem for tortoises in some areas, but this is highly controversial.

• *Poaching* removes an unknown number of tortoises from the wild, especially near urban areas. When too many tortoises are taken, those remaining may have difficulty finding mates.

Some misguided people even use tortoises for target practice! But there are also many people who feel a special affection for tortoises, and there is ongoing research aimed at tortoise preservation. You can help, too, by spreading understanding of these gentle and intelligent creatures and the laws protecting them.

Related questions:

Q2. Why is the Sonoran Desert so hot and dry?
Q8. Are saguaros endangered?

QUESTION 37

How can I avoid dangerous encounters with rattlers and Gila monsters?

ANSWER: *Always pay attention to where you're going, and use a flashlight at night.*

Rattlesnakes will strike at you only if they're molested or startled, so if you don't plan to bother them your task is simply to avoid making a sudden and unexpected appearance in their immediate vicinity. As for Gila monsters, you practically have to put your hand or foot on them to get bitten.

Here's some specific advice.

• Stay on the trail, or if you must go off-trail, try to avoid tall grass or brush.

Rattlesnakes and Gila monsters are beautifully camouflaged, and they're especially hard to see in places like this.

• As you walk, keep your eyes not just on the path but also on the area beside it. Desert bird watching and mountain gazing are fine, but best not done on the move. (Walking into a cactus is no fun, either.)

• Never put your feet or hands (or any other feature of your anatomy) where you can't see. Look on the other side of a rock or log before you step over it, and be sure to check all around one before you sit on it.

• Use a flashlight even in twilight or bright moonlight. Light that's sufficient to see where you're going may be too dim to distinguish a rattlesnake from a stick or a crack in the rock.

• Be aware of reptile habits. Rattlesnakes and Gila monsters may be sunning themselves in the open on cool days and moving about on warm days, but when it's hot they're more likely to be resting under rocks, bushes or logs. Warm nights are prime hunting hours for rattlesnakes, but the Gila monsters have mostly gone to bed.

Be cautious, but don't worry. Rattlers and Gila monsters don't lie in wait for hapless humans. Their first line of defense is simply to be inconspicuous: hikers often walk right past them without knowing it. (Perhaps that isn't reassuring!) Still, if you hike in the desert often, sooner or later you'll have the pleasure of meeting a rattlesnake or a Gila monster along the trail.

• What should I do if I come across a rattlesnake or Gila monster?

Count yourself lucky! You have a chance to observe one of the desert's most exciting creatures in the wild.

If you hear a rattlesnake rattle (or think you do), stop, look around for the snake, then step carefully away from it. Try not to jump without looking where you're going—you may land in a prickly pear, or even on another snake. If you spot a silent rattlesnake or a Gila monster, back off carefully, too.

Once you're at a safe distance you can enjoy watching the creature. How close is safe? Rattlesnakes can't strike farther than their own body length, and Gila monsters can manage a short lunge at best, so ten

DON'T TREAD ON ME

If the message sent by a rattling rattlesnake could be put into words, it might be this: "I'm here and I'm dangerous." Anyone who's received this message knows how persuasive it can be! The snake sends this warning not for your sake, but for its own, to protect itself from a potential predator or a large animal that might step on it. It has nothing to do with how the snake captures its own prey.

Rattlesnakes often hunt by day, and some take lizards, frogs, and toads, but they're especially well adapted to capture warm-blooded prey at night. A rattlesnake uses two heat-sensitive pits near its nostrils to locate the warm body of an unfortunate nocturnal rodent. (That's why it's called a "pit viper.") The pits work like infrared cameras, allowing the snake to "see" in the dark.

The rattlesnake strikes—a quick stabbing motion to inject venom with its hypodermic fangs—and the rodent wanders off until it's immobilized. Then, using its nose and tongue, the snake follows the scent trail left by its dying prey. With every flick, its forked tongue picks up odor particles which are sensed by special sensitive structures (**Jacobson's organs**) in the roof of its mouth.

At the end of the trail awaits the meal, already being digested by enzymes in the venom, and ready to be swallowed whole, head-first.

feet is certainly far enough, and it buys you time for cautious retreat if the animal happens to move toward you while looking for a hiding place.

> *Tarantulas are another good reason to use a flashlight at night—but only because they're too interesting to miss! These gentle creatures don't bite unless seriously provoked, and their venom isn't dangerous. However, they also deter predators (and threatening humans) by rubbing their legs across their abdomen and flinging irritating barbed hairs into the air, so enjoy them from a few feet away. Look for tarantulas at night during the monsoon, when males leave their burrows to wander the desert, searching for mates.*

It should go without saying, but don't molest the animal or try to pick it up. More than half of all venomous reptile bites are "illegitimate"—they happen when someone harasses or tries to grab the animal. Above all, don't injure or kill a rattlesnake or Gila monster—or any reptile, for that matter. They're part of what makes our desert so interesting. (And Gila monsters and certain rattlesnakes are protected by law.)

In the unlikely event that you're bitten, you'll want to know in advance what to do. You'll find that information in Appendix C.

Related questions:

Q25. What kind of snake is in my yard?
Q26. How can I keep rattlesnakes out of my yard?
Q30. What might I bring on a hike to help me enjoy the desert?
Q31. What precautions should I take when hiking in the desert?
Q35. How dangerous are Sonoran Desert toads?
Q38. Are there other venomous reptiles in the Sonoran Desert?
See also Appendix C: Venomous Bites and Stings.

QUESTION

Are there other venomous reptiles in the Sonoran Desert?

ANSWER: *The western coral snake is the only other reptile in the American Southwest with a venom dangerous to people.*

The western coral snake (*Micruroides euryxanthus*) is a small, shiny snake with red, yellow, and black bands around its body. Its venom is highly toxic, but its tiny mouth makes it difficult for it to bite a creature as large as you, and it's extremely unlikely even to try unless it's handled. You may hike in the desert for decades and never see a coral snake. An encounter with one of these beautiful and secretive creatures is an occasion to savor, not to fear.

The western coral snake's bright bands are warning colors (**aposematic** markings)—they serve notice that the snake is dangerous. Interestingly, there are several harmless desert snakes with colors similar to the coral snake's. Their markings may fool potential predators into thinking these snakes are dangerous, too. The evolution of living things that look (or sound or smell) like others for deceptive purposes is called **mimicry,** and it has happened many times in animals and plants.

♦ *How can I tell the Western coral snake from its mimics?*

Coral snake mimics look enough like the real thing to confuse not only predators, but human beings, too. Many people believe that red and yellow markings touch each other on coral snakes but not on harmless look-alikes. ("Red on yellow,

Western coral snake

SHORT IN THE TOOTH

Rattlesnakes and coral snakes have their fangs in the front of the upper jaw. Rattlesnake fangs are long and hollow, and they fold away neatly when the mouth is closed, while western coral snake fangs are smaller, solid, and immovable.

In the American Southwest there are also several very mildly venomous snakes with small fangs in the rear of the upper jaw. They're nothing to worry about. Most of them are small creatures and disinclined to bite even if you pick them up. Their venom isn't dangerous; it usually causes nothing more than a stinging or burning sensation and perhaps local swelling, and requires only minimal first aid, if any.

You may enjoy looking up these interesting "rearfanged" snakes in a good field guide (several are suggested in the bibliography). They're listed below.

Lyre snake
(Trimorphodon biscutatus)

Brown vine snake
(Oxybelis aeneus)

Black-headed snakes
(Tantilla species)

Night snake
(Hypsiglena torquata)

Ringneck snake
(Diadophis punctatus)

Western hognose snake
(Heterodon nasicus)

kill a fellow; red on black, friend of Jack.") But some harmless snakes have red and yellow in contact, too, and an occasional western coral snake has almost no red visible from above!

Here are some field marks that will help to identify western coral snakes. Each of these characteristics by itself is shared by some other snakes, but only the coral snake has them all.

• *Small.* Usually as thin as a pencil and less than 15 inches long (but occasionally more than 20 inches long).

• *Black head.*

• *Colored bands in this repeating sequence: yellow, red, yellow, black...* The "yellow" bands may actually be cream or white, and some individuals have black flecks or spots partly covering the red bands.

• *Colored bands completely encircling the body.*

Fortunately, you don't have to remember all this to avoid being bitten by a coral snake. You can always let the mimics have their way: just don't pick up any snake marked in red, yellow, and black!

In the exceedingly unlikely event you ever need to give first aid for a western coral snake bite, you'll find the treatment in Appendix C.

Related questions:

Q25. What kind of snake is in my yard?
Q26. How can I keep rattlesnakes out of my yard?
Q37. How can I avoid dangerous encounters with rattlers and Gila monsters?
See also Appendix C: Venomous Bites and Stings.

QUESTION

What is valley fever?

ANSWER: *Valley fever is a usually mild (but sometimes serious) disease caused by a fungus that lives in desert soils.*

Valley fever, technically called **coccidioidomycosis,** or cocci (KOK-see) for short, is caused by the soil fungus *Coccidioides immitis.* (See sidebar, page 119). Microscopic spores produced by the fungus are released into the air when the ground is disturbed, and they can infect people who inhale them. Some wild and domestic animals can get cocci, too. Cocci isn't contagious: you can't catch it from an infected person or animal.

Cocci occurs in the Sonoran, Mohave, and Chihuahuan Deserts of the United States and Mexico, as well as in the drier parts of Central and South America. It's not completely confined to desert areas; people living in the semiarid areas bordering deserts can be infected as well.

Evidence of valley fever has been detected in an Indian skeleton more than a thousand years old. The fungus is common in ancient Indian middens—a minor hazard that "comes with the territory" for Southwestern archaeologists.

The disease is especially common in the San Joaquin Valley of California—that's how it got the name "valley fever"—and in southern Arizona.

◆ What are the symptoms?

Almost all cocci infections are confined to the lungs. The effects are often so mild that people have no idea they have the disease. A majority of infections go unnoticed or seem like slight colds. Most of the rest are flulike, with symptoms like fever, tiredness, chest pains, aching joints, headaches, and coughing. There may be rashes or painful bumps on the skin. Some of these symptoms can linger for months and be quite unpleasant, but they're usually not dangerous.

> *Valley fever is quite common in dogs, but curiously rare in cats. Infected dogs often show fever, listlessness, loss of appetite, and cough; sometimes lameness, too. If your dog has these symptoms, see a veterinarian. If valley fever is diagnosed, medication will probably be necessary.*

Most of the truly serious cases are among the 1 or 2% of infections that spread beyond the lungs, most commonly to the skin, bones, and joints. The occasional deaths from cocci mostly happen when the infection spreads to the membranes covering the brain. Fortunately,

effective treatments are usually available and deaths from cocci are rare.

◆ What should I do if I suspect I have valley fever?

Because for most people cocci seems so much like a cold or flu, you can't tell by the symptoms alone that you have the disease. However, if you develop these symptoms at a hot, dry time of year—which is when the spores are usually spread—and especially within three weeks after breathing an unusual amount of desert dust, you should suspect cocci. If your symptoms are troublesome or long-lasting, see a doctor.

Usually the human immune system can handle a cocci infection by itself, and no special treatment is needed. It's mostly the unusual cases that spread beyond the lungs that require treatment. Because cocci is more likely to spread in pregnant women and people with diabetes, Hodgkin's disease, or HIV (AIDS virus) infection, and in people whose immune systems are suppressed by certain drug therapies, their cases always warrant special attention.

◆ How can I avoid getting valley fever?

Short of packing up and leaving the desert or permanently holding your breath (not recommended), there's no way to make sure you'll never get cocci. Most infections probably stem from a single inhaled spore! Still, it's worth avoiding heavy exposure to desert dust, because cases where many spores are inhaled tend to be more severe.

Try not to breathe large amounts of airborne dust, especially in the hot, dry months. Stay indoors or roll up automobile windows during dust storms. Wet down the soil before potentially dust-raising activities, like digging. Avoid dust from vehicles on dirt roads and minimize

off-road driving—which is unhealthy for the desert, as well as for you.

If you've never had cocci, and you live in a place where the fungus is prevalent, your chances of getting it are about one in thirty each year. If you're an adult who has grown up in the Sonoran Desert there's a good chance you've already had cocci—and that you didn't know it at the time.

◆ Can I catch cocci more than once?

Fortunately, once your body has successfully fought off a cocci infection you're immune—you can't catch it again. If you'd like to find out whether you're already a cocci veteran, you can ask your doctor for a skin test.

Some day there may be a vaccine and people won't have to contract the disease to become immune. When that happens we desert dwellers will be able to breathe a little easier. In the meantime, valley fever is a small risk we take to live in a beautiful place.

Related questions:

Q2. Why is the Sonoran Desert so hot and dry?
Q3. Are there seasons in the Sonoran Desert?
Q40. What precautions should I take when driving in the desert?
See also Appendix D: Hantavirus.

THE FUNGUS AMONG US

Coccidioides immitis, the soil organism responsible for valley fever, can't be seen with the unaided eye. It's a fungus—a distant relative of mushrooms and puffballs, the yeast in your bread, and the fuzz that grows on food left too long in the refrigerator. But it's one as desert-adapted as a saguaro or a sidewinder: it thrives in **alkaline** soils and absolutely requires a climate that cycles dramatically between cool-moist and hot-dry.

Coccidioides depends on the desert sun to bake and sterilize the upper soil during a period of drought. When the next rainy season arrives the fungus grows rapidly, spreading upward into the biological vacuum, outcompeting other fungi less tolerant of alkaline soils. When the ground dries out again it produces its tiny spores, ready to be launched into the air by a dust storm, automobile tire, or bulldozer.

New valley fever cases reflect this cycle. In Arizona, with two rainy periods, most people are infected in the dry foresummer and fall. In California, with only one rainy season, valley fever season extends right through the summer without a monsoon break.

What precautions should I take when driving in the desert?

ANSWER: *Take care of both vehicle and driver, and use common sense.*

Highway travel in the Southwest has come a long way since the days when trembling stagecoach passengers relinquished their watches to *bandidos* in black hats—but it still pays to be careful!

• Carry water with you. On a long trip in hot weather you might need it for both yourself and the radiator. Bring a large cup to sip even for a short trip around town in an air-conditioned car. You'll be very glad to have it if a tire goes flat.

• Keep your vehicle in good condition. Pay extra attention to the tires and anything having to do with engine cooling— the fan belt, oil level, and radiator. Don't forget that "antifreeze" does more than keep radiators from bursting in Minnesota in December; it also keeps them from boiling over in Arizona in July.

• On long trips in very hot weather, consider driving at night and sleeping by day. But if the star-lit landscape makes you sleepy behind the wheel, pull over and take a nap.

• Gas stations can be few and very far between on some desert highways. Always make sure you have enough in your tank to reach the next one.

• Beware of heat-crazed motorists. Hot weather can fray nerves as quickly as fan belts, so adjust your courtesy level upward with the thermometer.

• Any special advice for back-road travel?

• Think of back-road desert driving as something like desert hiking on wheels, and take similar precautions. Let someone

kit and pump; jack and a one-foot-square piece of heavy plywood to put under it on soft ground; jumper cables; fire extinguisher; shovel.

• Don't go places unsuited to your automobile. A low-clearance vehicle on a rutted and rocky road may result in a bigger driving adventure than you bargained for.

• Beware of soft sand. It can take seconds to get stuck in a dune or a wash, but hours to get unstuck. If you think the way might be treacherous, stop, get out, and try it on foot. If it's questionable, don't take the chance.

OFFENSIVE DRIVING

The desert's wide-open spaces can be a temptation to people who like to drive off-road. If you feel the urge to spin your wheels among the creosote bushes, stop, set your brake and consider the consequences.

Tire tracks can disfigure a desert landscape for many decades, but the damage goes far beyond appearances. Desert plants injured by automobiles are slow to recover, depriving desert animals of precious food and shelter. Animal burrows are easily crushed, and sometimes their inhabitants with them.

The damage doesn't stop when you pull back on the road. Fragile soil crusts (**cryptobiotic soils**) are completely destroyed by automobile wheels, opening the ground to long-term erosion by wind and water. (See Question 41 sidebar, page 125.) And your tracks are likely to encourage others to follow you, initiating a vicious cycle of escalating destruction.

No one says you must confine your wheels to pavement, but there are enough rugged dirt roads in the desert backcountry to test anyone's driving skill. If these don't satisfy your urge to explore, it may be time to turn off the ignition and lace up your hiking boots.

know where you're going and when you expect to return, and if possible travel with a companion in a second vehicle.

• Bring a generous supply of water and several quarts of oil.

• Carry a good set of tools and extra parts. These should be on your list: spare tire, fan belt, and radiator hose; tire repair

• How can I tell whether or not it's safe to drive across a flooded wash?

You can't. Drivers who thought they could are regularly shown on local television newscasts, clinging to vehicles surrounded by rushing water—yet people keep trying to beat the odds!

Since water flows so infrequently in desert **washes** and **arroyos,** engineers often save the expense of a bridge and allow a road to dip to the level of the usually dry streambed. Don't drive through a flooded crossing. Not only might the water be deeper than you suspect, and its force stronger than you imagine, but moving sand and gravel under the water is treacherous "footing" for any vehicle. It's like walking on marbles in a hurricane. And if the water is deep enough, buoyancy will lift your car right off the ground.

If you don't drown, you may wish you had when you're presented with a bill for the rescue!

◆ *What should I do if I'm caught in a blinding dust storm?*

Pull off the road as far as possible, park, turn off the lights, and take your foot off the brake pedal. Drivers seeing red tail-lights in a dust storm have been known to mistake stopped vehicles for moving ones and try to follow them— with disastrous results.

Two conditions are necessary to produce a dust storm. The first, of course, is wind. A moving wall of dust can result when cold air falls out of the bottom of a summer thunderstorm and spills outward, creating a powerful local wind called a "haboob." More widespread strong winds can also raise dust; these are more common in winter and spring. The second condition is loose soil for the wind to pick up. Agricultural fields, other areas cleared of natural vegetation, and dry lakebeds are all frequent contributors.

Incidentally, dust storms are ideal conditions for spreading the fungal spores that cause valley fever, so stay in the car with the windows rolled up until it's safe to drive on. (See Question 39.)

Related questions:

Q30. What might I bring on a hike to help me enjoy the desert?
Q31. What precautions should I take when hiking in the desert?
Q39. What is valley fever?
Q41. How can I minimize my impact on the desert?

QUESTION

How can I minimize my impact on the desert?

ANSWER: *You can begin by taking only memories and leaving only footprints.*

This often-repeated saying has special meaning in a desert, where plant and animal life is sparse and the land is slow to heal.

"Take only memories" means resisting the natural human impulse to collect beautiful objects. An unpicked wildflower feeds pollinators now and—thanks to the seeds it will produce—in future years as well. Left alone, an animal bone will be gnawed by desert rodents to recover its calcium. Feathers and cactus skeletons, too, will eventually be broken down and recycled into living plants and animals.

Even interesting stones should be left for others of your own species to enjoy. And, of course, prehistoric and historic artifacts should stay as you find them. If you'd like a reminder of your discoveries, consider taking photographs, making sketches, or keeping a journal. (See Question 42.)

In the desert, "leave only footprints" should probably be amended with "and as few of those as possible!" Stay on trails when you're hiking, or if you must go off-trail, try to put your feet where they're least likely to do harm: on stones where they'll leave no marks, or in sandy washes where they'll more quickly be erased. Try to avoid stepping on plants or the living crusts called **cryptobiotic soils.** (See sidebar, page 125.)

Your automobile leaves even larger footprints than you do, so it's important to keep your tires on the road. Unfortunately, some off-road vehicle enthusiasts

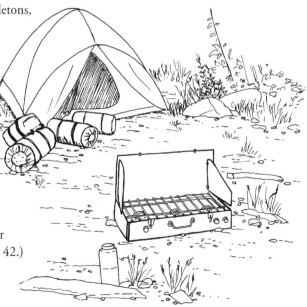

consider the desert their playground. Needless to say, this can be a terribly destructive form of recreation. (See Question 40 sidebar, page 121.)

• Are there other things I can do to keep from disturbing desert wildlife?

Watch active bird nests from a distance rather than approaching or touching them. While it isn't true that birds will abandon nests because of odors you leave (most birds have an even worse sense of smell than we do), your odor trail is quite likely to be detected by the sensitive nose of a coyote or a fox. It may lead the curious predator straight to a meal.

> Cooking on a camp stove instead of a fire befits an attitude of self-sufficiency that can guide your desert camping. Instead of thinking of the desert as a source of things you can use along the way—fuel, water, and food— bring with you everything you need (and take it all away afterwards). Leave the desert's limited resources for the wild things that truly need them.

If you come across a deer fawn without its mother, don't disturb it. It's quite normal for a doe to leave her young alone for hours while she goes off to forage. Fawns "kidnapped" by well-meaning hikers can

seldom be returned to the wild. Likewise, baby rabbits and well-feathered young birds away from nests or parents are seldom abandoned. (See Question 20.)

The desert's rare water holes are especially precious to wildlife. No matter how hot the day, resist the powerful temptation to jump in and cool off. How would you like it if someone bathed in *your* drinking water supply?

It also helps just to be quiet out there. Not only will excessive noise disturb animals, the desert's quiet is something wonderful in itself—enjoy it! Incidentally, quiet is much easier to maintain if you hike in small groups, which are less apt to disturb the desert in other ways, too.

• Any special recommendations for campers?

In the desert, as elsewhere, it's a good idea to camp in established sites whenever possible, to avoid trampling or clearing new areas. If you must occupy a pristine site, choose an unvegetated spot with resistant ground—like rock or gravel— and do your best to leave no trace of your stay. And, of course, keep your campsite away from nesting areas, natural water sources, and other sensitive places.

While gazing into an evening campfire is part of the romance of the outdoors for many people, it's a pastime ill-suited to desert camping. Organic material isn't abundant in a desert, and fallen wood is critical to animals that live on, under, and inside it, or, like termites, feed upon it. Use a small gas- or gasoline-fueled camp stove instead, and try spending the after-dinner hours enjoying the starry desert sky.

Human wastes can be disposed of in the usual way: by digging a hole about six

THE DESERT'S UPPER CRUST

They're easy to overlook but surprisingly important: the dark, lumpy crusts on the surfaces of many desert soils. Called **cryptobiotic soils** or **cryptogamic crusts**, they're actually entire communities of microscopic organisms—bacteria, algae, fungi, mosses, and the tiny creatures that eat them.

The most important members of these miniature communities are **cyanobacteria** (often called "blue-green algae"). Not only are these self-sufficient organisms capable of making their own food by **photosynthesis**, they also have the rare ability to "fix" nitrogen gas from the air by changing it to a form they and other organisms can use. They're thus perfect "pioneer" species for colonizing barren soil surfaces, and their ancestors may have been among the first living things to move onto the land hundreds of millions of years ago.

Nitrogen fixed by cyanobacteria fertilizes nutrient-poor desert soils, is taken up by the roots of plants, and eventually nourishes the animals that feed upon them. Sticky substances secreted by these bacteria absorb rainwater like a sponge, and glue together soil particles, forming a protective crust over the soil. This fragile living surface is easily damaged by trampling, opening the soil to erosion by wind and water. It can take decades to recover.

inches deep. This can be a chore in a rocky desert soil, but it's better than taking the easy way out by digging in the loose sand of a wash.

◆ Anything else?

Yes. Take care of yourself. If you go into the desert well prepared and pay attention to your own body's needs and limitations, you're far less likely to find yourself in an emergency situation. A search and rescue team would leave far more footprints than would you alone!

Related questions:

Q1. What exactly is a desert?
Q20. What should I do about an injured, sick, or orphaned animal in my yard?
Q30. What might I bring on a hike to help me enjoy the desert?
Q31. What precautions should I take when hiking in the desert?
Q34. Why don't I see very many animals when I hike in the desert?
Q36. If I find a desert tortoise, would it be all right to take it home as a pet?
Q40. What precautions should I take when driving in the desert?
Q42. What else can I do to explore the desert?

What else can I do to explore the desert?

ANSWER: *Visit many places, but get to know at least one of them well.*

We're fortunate that so many interesting Sonoran Desert habitats are in public ownership. These places belong to us, and it's worth seeing as many of them as we can. Don't limit yourself to National Parks and Monuments; visit National Wildlife Refuges, National Forests, and National Recreation Areas, as well as state and local parks. But take your time—you don't have to see them all in one year! You'll find it much more enjoyable to spend several days exploring each one than to rush from one to the next.

Exploring far and wide is a wonderful part of getting to know the desert, but many people find their greatest satisfaction in becoming intimate with a single place. Your favorite location needn't be a large area or far away—perhaps just an interesting trail a few minutes from home, or even

Black-chinned hummingbird

a desert backyard. Visit it again and again. Look for the blooming cactus, the black beetle, and the bobcat's track. Watch the winter storm and the rising moon. When the rocks start to seem like old friends, your best explorations may be just beginning.

◆ What can I do to help me learn about new places I visit?

Don't wait until you arrive. Write ahead for free pamphlets. (Look for addresses in the organizations list at the back of this book.) Descriptive guide-books have been published for many parks, monuments, and recreation areas—check your bookstore or library. If you can do some reading in advance, you'll be prepared to make the most of your visit.

Another strategy is to make your visit with someone more knowledgeable than you. Many special interest clubs, such as native plant societies and local Audubon Society chapters, sponsor frequent field trips for their members. Some nature centers and museums (including the Arizona-Sonora Desert Museum) do the same. You might wish to join one or more of these organizations both for the benefits of their collective knowledge and for the fun of exploring with others who share your interests.

◆ What can I do to help me remember what I've experienced and learned?

Consider keeping a journal. It would give you a meaningful reminder of your experiences—without the need for collecting—and would be a valuable way to organize your thoughts. And your

well-recorded observations might even make a scientific contribution!

Journal keeping should be a pleasure, not a chore. Your journal could be written to share with others, or it could be private, like a personal diary. Some people like to write directly in their journals as things happen. Others prefer to scribble quick notes on cards or in pocket notebooks during the day, then compose their journal entries after supper. This evening ritual can be a pleasant way to reflect on the day's experiences.

HINTS FOR NOTE TAKERS IN THE FIELD

1. Keep your notebook within reach. You'll be much more inclined to use it if it's in an accessible pocket than if you have to excavate it from your daybag.

2. Use a pencil with a clip. It won't run out of ink, it won't smear in the rain, and if you're lucky it may still be in your pocket at the end of the day!

Find your own way of taking notes. Why limit yourself to words? Try sketching—you don't have to be an artist! If perfectionist tendencies slow you down, try "minute sketching": allow only sixty seconds per drawing. Photographs can be pasted into a journal, too.

Recording sounds in a notebook is a real challenge. Try showing the ups and downs of bird songs with wiggly lines. These informal "sonograms" can be a very valuable memory aid. You could even carry a small tape recorder for sound "snapshots." It's up to you—enjoy yourself!

◆ *Any other advice?*

Yes: never stop learning about the desert. Read all you can, attend lectures, visit museums, surf the Internet—find information wherever you can. The more you learn, the more you'll realize how much more is left to discover—and the more meaningful your explorations will be.

As you become more knowledgeable, you may feel the desire to share what you know. As anyone who's had the experience will tell you, one of the best ways to learn is to teach someone else. Why not volunteer at a local school, nature center, or museum? Many parks, monuments, and national forests have volunteer programs, too. There's real satisfaction in helping others learn about things that are important to you. And by spreading the word

about the beauty and intricacy of the Sonoran Desert, you'll help to make sure that future generations have the pleasure of exploring it, too.

Related questions:

Q30. What might I bring on a hike to help me enjoy the desert?
Q31. What precautions should I take when hiking in the desert?
Q34. Why don't I see very many animals when I hike in the desert?
Q40. What precautions should I take when driving in the desert?
Q41. How can I minimize my impact on the desert?

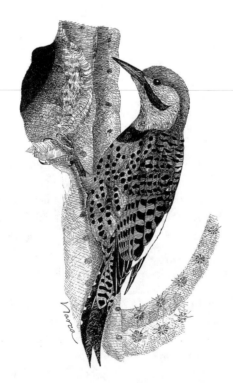

Gilded flicker

Additional Information

Appendix A: CLIMATE

This appendix lists temperatures and rainfall at four Sonoran Desert cities. Tucson and Phoenix are located in the Arizona Upland subdivision of the Sonoran Desert. Yuma and Palm Springs are in the Lower Colorado River Valley subdivision. (For more about the subdivisions of the Sonoran Desert, see the Introduction and Question 2.)

Averages are for the years 1961-90. Temperatures are Fahrenheit, rounded to the nearest degree. Precipitation is in inches, rounded to the nearest tenth. The last column is annual averages.

Records are for 1948-96 for the Arizona cities; 1927-96 for Palm Springs. Precipitation figures are rounded as above.

TUCSON, ARIZONA (elevation 2,390 feet)

Average	Jan	Feb	Mar	Apr	May	Jun	Jul	Aug	Sep	Oct	Nov	Dec	*Annual*
High	64°	68°	73°	81°	90°	100°	99°	97°	93°	84°	73°	64°	82°
Low	39°	41°	45°	50°	58°	68°	74°	72°	68°	57°	46°	40°	55°
Precip	0.9	0.7	0.7	0.3	0.2	0.2	2.4	2.2	1.7	1.1	0.7	1.1	12.0

Record high temperature: 117°F (26 June 1990)   *Record wet year:* 21.9 inches (1983)
Record low temperature: 16°F (4 January 1949)   *Record dry year:* 5.3 inches (1953)

PHOENIX, ARIZONA (elevation 1,090 feet)

Average	Jan	Feb	Mar	Apr	May	Jun	Jul	Aug	Sep	Oct	Nov	Dec	*Annual*
High	66°	71°	76°	85°	94°	104°	106°	104°	98°	88°	75°	66°	86°
Low	41°	45°	49°	55°	64°	73°	81°	79°	73°	61°	49°	42°	59°
Precip	0.7	0.7	0.9	0.2	0.1	0.1	0.8	1.0	0.9	0.7	0.7	1.0	7.7

Record high temperature: 122°F (26 June 1990)   *Record wet year:* 15.2 inches (1978)
Record low temperature: 17°F (5 January 1950)   *Record dry year:* 2.8 inches (1956)

YUMA, ARIZONA (elevation 160 feet)

Average	Jan	Feb	Mar	Apr	May	Jun	Jul	Aug	Sep	Oct	Nov	Dec	*Annual*
High	69°	74°	79°	86°	94°	103°	107°	105°	101°	90°	77°	69°	88°
Low	44°	47°	51°	57°	64°	72°	81°	80°	73°	62°	51°	44°	61°
Precip	0.4	0.2	0.2	0.1	0.0	0.0	0.3	0.6	0.3	0.3	0.2	0.5	3.2

Record high temperature: 124°F (28 July 1995)   *Record wet year:* 6.8 inches (1989)
Record low temperature: 24°F (8 January 1971)   *Record dry year:* 0.3 inches (1956)

PALM SPRINGS, CALIFORNIA (elevation 475 feet)

Average	Jan	Feb	Mar	Apr	May	Jun	Jul	Aug	Sep	Oct	Nov	Dec	*Annual*
High	70°	75°	80°	87°	95°	104°	109°	107°	101°	91°	79°	70°	89°
Low	43°	46°	49°	54°	61°	68°	75°	75°	68°	60°	49°	42°	58°
Precip	1.0	0.8	0.5	0.1	0.1	0.1	0.2	0.4	0.4	0.2	0.7	0.7	5.2

Record high temperature: 123°F (10 July 1979)   *Record wet year:* 18.6 inches (1943)
Record low temperature: 19°F (22 January 1937)   *Record dry year:* 1.0 inches (1956)

Appendix B: HUMMINGBIRD GARDENS

The easiest way to invite hummingbirds to your garden is simply to put out a feeder (see Question 18), but you might prefer a more "natural" approach: offering them plants that provide food and cover. The initial investment in time, money, and labor is larger, but the dividends in satisfaction are great.

There are several advantages to the landscaping strategy.

1. Hummingbird flowers are attractive to people, too. You'll enjoy their beauty even when the hummingbirds are busy elsewhere.

2. Though no garden is maintenance-free, you might find caring for plants and soil more pleasant than the repetitive routine of mixing sugar water and cleaning feeders.

3. Your landscaping will provide a bonus by drawing other interesting wildlife, including insects and other birds. Some of the insects will be additional hummingbird food. Webs built by spiders to catch the insects will be hummingbird nest material. You won't just be feeding hummingbirds; you'll be creating a hummingbird-friendly ecosystem!

The two charts in this appendix can help you get started. The first gives examples of plants hummingbirds will use for roosting. Although hummers are most often noticed in flight, they actually spend most of their day resting. They prefer low, evergreen bushes and trees that are moderately dense, with horizontal branching. If you're lucky, hummingbirds may nest in these plants, too. You may want to encourage them by putting out nesting materials such as animal fur, plant down, cotton thread, strips of tissue, or clothes dryer lint.

The second chart lists plants with flowers suitable for hummingbird feeding. All have been tested in the Hummingbird Aviary at the Arizona-Sonora Desert Museum. Since there are hummingbirds in the Sonoran Desert year-round, it makes sense to choose a selection that will provide flowers in every season. (For more about the special characteristics of hummingbird flowers see Question 18, sidebar, page 57.)

Hummingbirds seem to enjoy bathing, so consider providing water as well. Moving or dripping water is best. Not only do the hummers prefer it, it's also less likely to spread disease.

You'll find more information on hummingbird gardening in some of the books listed in Appendix G under Question 18: How can I attract hummingbirds?

ROOSTING PLANTS FOR HUMMINGBIRDS

Scientific name	Common name
Berberis haematocarpa	Barberry
Heteromeles arbutifolia	Toyon
Ilex vomitoria	Yaupon holly
Leucophyllum frutescens	Texas ranger
Prunus ilicifolia	Holly-leaved cherry
Rhamnus californica	California buckthorn
Rhus choriophylla	Sumac
Simmondsia chinensis	Jojoba
Vauquelinia californica	Arizona rosewood

FOOD PLANTS FOR HUMMINGBIRDS

Scientific name	Common name	Flower color	Flowering season
Aloe barbadensis	Aloe vera	yellow or reddish	Spring
Aloe karasburgensis	Aloe	reddish-pink	Summer, Fall
Anisacanthus andersonii		reddish	Winter, Spring
Anisacanthus quadrifidus	Desert honeysuckle	orange	Summer, Fall
Aquilegia chrysantha	Yellow columbine	yellow	Spring
Bouvardia glaberrima	Bouvardia	red	Spring, Summer
Calliandra californica	Baja fairy duster	red	Year-round*
Calliandra eriophylla	Fairy duster	pink	Spring
Cirsium arizonicum	Arizona thistle	red	Summer
Erythrina flabelliformis	Coral bean	red	Spring
Galvezia juncea	Galvezia	red	Year-round*
Hesperaloe nocturna	White hesperaloe	cream	Spring
Hesperaloe parviflora	Red hesperaloe	pink	Spring
Heuchera sanguinea	Coral bells	pink to red	Spring, Summer
Justicia candicans	Red jacobinia	red	Spring, Fall, Winter*
Justicia sonorae		purple	Spring
Justicia spicigera	Orange jacobinia	orange	Year-round*
Lobelia cardinalis	Cardinal flower	red	Summer
Lobelia laxiflora	Lobelia	red	Spring
Mammilaria setispina		red	Summer
Maurandya antirrhiniflora	Snapdragon vine	blue or red	Spring, Summer, Fall
Mimulus cardinalis	Crimson monkey flower	red	Spring, Summer, Fall
Pedilanthus macrocarpus	Candelilla	red	Summer
Salvia davidsonii	Sage	red	Spring, Fall, Winter
Salvia elegans	Pineapple sage	red	Summer, Fall, Winter*
Salvia greggii	Autumn sage	red or pink	Spring, Summer, Fall
Salvia lemmonii		pink	Spring, Summer, Fall
Salvia mohavensis	Mohave sage	blue	Spring
Salvia mohavensis x *clevelandii*	"Carl Nielsen" sage	blue	Spring
Stenocereus alamosensis	Sina	reddish	Summer
Tecoma stans	Yellow bells	yellow	Summer, Fall
Zauschneria californica	Hummingbird trumpet	red	Summer, Fall
Zauschneria cana	Hummingbird trumpet	red	Summer, Winter

* If winter temperatures don't drop below freezing, or if plant is protected

Appendix C: VENOMOUS BITES AND STINGS

This appendix gives symptoms and recommended management of venomous bites and stings by certain Sonoran Desert animals. Only the most dangerous, painful, or feared bites and stings are included. For more comprehensive lists of venomous species, consider references given under Questions 21, 22, 37, and 38 in Appendix G.

All the bites and stings listed here warrant attention, but not undue alarm. Deaths from bites and stings are rare in the United States. In the Sonoran Desert in Arizona and California, as elsewhere in the country, the venomous creature causing the greatest number of deaths is the honey bee—not because it's rapidly becoming Africanized, but because of severe allergic reactions in sensitized persons. (See sidebar, page 137.)

Check with a physician about the need for a tetanus booster after a bite or sting. Any puncture wound carries with it a small risk of tetanus infection.

If you have any questions, don't hesitate to call your state's poison control system:

• **Arizona Poison Control System**
  1-800-362-0101

• **California Poison Control System**
  1-800-876-4766

(Much of the following is taken directly from information published by the Arizona Poison and Drug Information Center. Used by permission.)

BARK SCORPION
(*Centruroides exilicauda*)
Identification: See Question 21. This is the only desert scorpion in Arizona or California whose sting is considered potentially life-threatening.
Symptoms of a sting:
  • Immediate pain at the site, with little swelling.
  • Often, numbness and tingling.
  • Often, extreme sensitivity to touch, pressure, heat, or cold at the site.
  • Small children are at highest risk. They may show hyperactivity, "roving eye," and respiratory difficulty.
  • Rarely, more severe whole-body reactions may occur, such as changes in heart rate and blood pressure.
What to do:
  1. Call your state poison control system.
  2. Most stings in healthy adults can be managed at home with basic first aid and follow-up. Clean the site with soap and water, apply a cool compress, elevate the stung limb to heart level, and give aspirin or acetaminophen (Tylenol®) as needed for minor discomfort.
  3. Any child who has been stung, or anyone experiencing severe symptoms should be taken to a health care facility immediately.

Stings by other species of scorpions usually cause only pain, swelling, and discoloration at the site. Treat them the same way.

For information about keeping bark scorpions out of your house, see Question 22.

BLACK WIDOW SPIDER
(*Latrodectus hesperus*)
Identification: See Question 21.
Symptoms of a bite:

• Often, immediate pain at the site, but little other local reaction.

• Later, pain, cramps, and rigidity may appear in the shoulders, back, chest, or abdomen.

• Sometimes nausea, vomiting, headache, or anxiety.

What to do:

1. Most bites in healthy adults can be managed at home. Clean the site with soap and water, apply a cool compress, elevate the bitten limb to the heart level, and give aspirin or acetaminophen (Tylenol®) for minor symptoms. Call your state poison control system for additional advice.

2. Children under 5 or any adult with severe symptoms may need treatment in a medical facility. The poison control system will advise you.

For information about keeping black widow spiders out of your house, see Question 22.

BROWN SPIDERS
(*Loxosceles* species)
Identification: See Question 21. The term "brown spiders" refers to a particular group of spiders; not all brown-colored spiders are members of this group.
Symptoms of a bite:

• Usually no immediate pain at the site. (The victim may not be aware of the bite.) However, pain may develop at the site in the first few hours.

• The site may become inflamed, with a blister developing a half day to several days after the bite. The blister will evolve into a "bulls-eye lesion" with a dark center (dead skin) outlined by white and set on a red and inflamed background. This can take months to heal and leave a serious scar.

• Flulike symptoms, including nausea, vomiting, fever, and malaise may appear during the first day.

What to do:

1. If you think you've been bitten by a brown spider, call your state poison control system.

2. Keep the site clean with soap and water to prevent infection.

3. Consult a physician. Medical treatment is always advised when a brown spider bite is suspected.

If you can do so safely, capture the spider to aid identification. Even a squashed specimen may be useful.

For information about keeping brown spiders out of your house, see Question 22.

TARANTULA
(*Aphonopelma* and *Dugesiella* species)
Identification: Large, hairy, slow-moving black to brown spiders, up to four inches long.
Symptoms of a bite:

• Seldom causes problems other than pain at the site (due partly to the large size of the fangs).

• A tarantula may also defend itself by brushing irritating, barbed hairs off its abdomen into the air. These hairs may cause itching, burning, and a rash.

What to do:

1. Clean the bite with soap and water and protect it against infection.

2. Remove the irritating hairs from your skin with cellophane tape or masking tape.

3. If you need additional information,

call your state poison control system.

For more about tarantulas, see Question 37 sidebar, page 114.

CENTIPEDES

Identification: Usually fast-moving arthropods with an elongated, flattened, segmented body and a single pair of legs on each segment. (Usually there are much fewer than the one hundred legs implied by the name.) The giant desert centipede, *Scolopendra heros,* grows to more than six inches long, and has blackish head and rear segments. Other species are smaller.

Symptoms of a bite:

• Pain and inflammation at the site, often lasting only a few hours. (There are cases where tenderness persists for several weeks, but these are extremely rare.)

What to do:

1. Many centipede bites can be treated at home. Encourage bleeding from the punctures, clean the site well with soap and water, and apply a cool compress.

2. A dilute ammonia solution (1 part household ammonia to 10 parts water), if applied early, has been reported to relieve local pain.

3. If pain is severe or lasts more than twelve hours, relief may be found in an emergency room or urgent care facility.

4. For additional information call your state poison control system.

CONENOSE BUGS

(*Triatoma* species)

Identification: See Question 28.

Symptoms of a bite:

• Typically, no pain is felt at the time of the bite.

• Later, pain, redness, swelling, and itching may develop at the site.

• Repeated bites may lead to sensitization, and all levels of allergic reaction are possible, including life-threatening anaphylaxis. (See sidebar, next page.)

What to do:

1. Call your state's poison control system.

2. Keep the bite site(s) clean with soap and water.

3. Antihistamines, dilute ammonia solutions (1 part household ammonia to ten parts ammonia), and bathing in Epsom salts (magnesium sulfate) may control itching.

4. A victim showing severe or whole body reactions during the first hour should be taken to a medical facility without delay.

5. If you've had a severe reaction, your doctor may prescribe an arthropod anaphylaxis kit.

For information about keeping conenose bugs out of your house, see Question 28.

HONEY BEE

(*Apis mellifera*)

Identification: There are several castes of honeybees in a colony, but most people only see the workers, which are so familiar they hardly require description. They are less than three-quarters of an inch long, covered with short hairs, with a dark head and thorax; the abdomen is sometimes quite dark as well. Africanized honey bees, which are members of the same species, look the same (and have the same venom).

Symptoms of a sting:

• Most people have local reactions: pain, redness, itching, and swelling at the

ANAPHYLAXIS

Anaphylaxis, also called anaphylactic shock, is a severe and sometimes fatal whole-body allergic reaction. It sometimes occurs in people who have become sensitized to bites by certain insects, including bees, wasps, conenose bugs, and harvester ants. Symptoms of anaphylaxis may include

1. Welts all over the body
2. Itching palms and feet
3. Headache
4. Nausea and vomiting
5. Labored breathing

A person experiencing anaphylaxis should be taken to a medical facility without delay. Dial 911.

Any person who has experienced a severe reaction to a bite or sting by an insect (or insect relative) should see a physician about a prescription for an arthropod anaphylaxis kit. The kit should be kept available at all times, both around town and on desert outings. The medications in the kit are an important first step in managing anaphylaxis, but the victim should still be taken to a medical facility immediately.

1. Quickly remove the stinger(s), as it (they) may still be pumping venom into the sting site. (It's okay to pull them out with your fingers. You don't need to scrape them off with a credit card, as has sometimes been recommended in the past.)

2. Clean the site(s) with soap and water.

3. A paste of baking soda and water, or meat tenderizer and water, followed by a cool compress, has been reported to minimize local reactions.

4. Closely observe how symptoms progress, especially during the first hour. Mild local symptoms may be relieved by taking antihistamines. Call your state poison control system if unusual or rapidly progressing symptoms occur. They may require aggressive life-support treatment at a health care facility.

A patient who has been stung more than fifteen times should be taken to a health care facility without delay. Pull out the stingers on the way.

Patients who show allergic sensitivity may be prescribed an emergency kit, which should be carried at all times. (See sidebar, this page.)

For more about Africanized honey bees, see Questions 23 and 24.

sting site, which may last several hours.

• People who have become sensitized (allergic) may have more severe reactions, even to a single sting: welts, itching palms and feet, headache, nausea, vomiting, and labored breathing. The most severe kind of allergic reaction, anaphylaxis, can be fatal. (See sidebar, this page.)

What to do:

If there have been fewer than fifteen stings:

ANTS
(including velvet ants)

Identification: Ordinary ants are easy to identify. All bite defensively. Some also spray formic acid on the bite, and some, such as harvester ants, sting. Velvet ants are actually wingless wasps, and they sting when molested. Their furry bodies can be black, yellow, orange, red, or white.

Symptoms of a bite or sting:
• Pain, swelling, and sometimes itching at the site are typical.

• Sensitized people may have allergic reactions, sometimes including anaphylaxis. (See sidebar, previous page.)

What to do:

1. Clean the site with soap and water and apply a cool compress.

2. A paste of baking soda and water or meat tenderizer and water may relieve some of the pain.

3. A victim showing severe or whole body reactions during the first hour after a bite or sting should be taken to medical facility without delay.

Don't hesitate to call your state poison control system for advice.

GILA MONSTER

(*Heloderma suspectum*)

Identification: A large, heavy-bodied lizard, sometimes more than twenty inches long, with beadlike scales and dark markings on a pink, orange, or yellow background. (Harmless banded geckos are sometimes mistaken for baby Gila monsters. See Question 26 sidebar, page 80.)

Symptoms of a bite:

• Severe pain, at first only at the site, but sometimes spreading.

• Sometimes swelling at the site, nausea, weakness, faintness, excessive perspiration, chills, and fever.

What to do:

1. Gila monsters have a well-deserved reputation for clamping down on a victim and not letting go. Disengage the lizard as quickly as possible. With the animal on the ground (not dangling, which would make it less likely to let go) place a strong stick between the bitten part and the back of the lizard's mouth, then push toward the rear of the jaw. If this doesn't work,

immerse the lizard in water. If water isn't available, grasp the lizard by the tail and yank it free.

2. Allow the wound to bleed freely, and irrigate it with plenty of water.

3. Immobilize the bitten limb at heart level.

4. Reassure the patient.

5. Take the patient to a health care facility.

For suggestions about avoiding Gila monster bites, see Question 37.

WESTERN CORAL SNAKE

(*Micruroides euryxanthus*)

Identification: See Question 38.

Symptoms of a bite:

• Minimal pain and swelling at the site.

• Symptoms are often delayed. Drowsiness, apprehension, giddiness, nausea, vomiting, and salivation can appear one to seven hours after the bite.

No deaths are known to have been caused by this species.

What to do:

First aid measures are of little value.

1. Withhold food, drink, and medication.

2. Take the victim to a medical facility without delay.

RATTLESNAKES

(*Crotalus* species)

Identification: See Question 25.

Symptoms of a bite:

Highly variable, depending on the species of rattlesnake, the quantity of venom injected, and other factors.

May include:

• Pain and swelling.

• Weakness, chills, or sweating.

- Numbness or tingling of the tongue, mouth, scalp, or feet.
- Dizziness or faintness.
- Nausea and vomiting.

Some rattlesnake bites are potentially fatal.

What to do:

Note: Certain first aid methods recommended in the past have only caused additional injury. *Do not* use ice, incision and suction, tourniquets, alcohol, drugs, or electric shock.

1. Calm and reassure the patient.

2. Remove any constricting items, such as jewelry, from the affected limb.

3. When practical, immobilize the limb at heart level.

4. Transport the patient to the nearest health care facility without delay.

5. Don't try to capture or kill the snake.

(It's dangerous, you'd delay transportation to professional care, and identifying the species of rattlesnake wouldn't significantly affect medical treatment.)

An additional first aid method can be safely used. Commercially available vacuum pump devices, sold in outdoor stores, have been shown to remove up to 30% of the venom if applied within three minutes of a bite. (These do not require incisions, and they apply much stronger suction than the rubber cups in the old "cut and suck" snakebite kits.) The pumps are useful and safe if used properly, but not sufficient in themselves to treat a venomous snakebite. Be sure also to take the steps listed above.

For suggestions about avoiding rattlesnake bites, see Questions 26 and 37.

Appendix D: HANTAVIRUS

This appendix mostly summarizes information on hantavirus published by the Centers for Disease Control and Prevention, U.S. Department of Health and Human Services. If you have any questions, especially concerning situations not covered here, don't hesitate to contact your local or state health departments. (See organizations list following appendixes and bibliography.)

Various hantaviruses infect rodents around the world, and some of these viruses can also infect human beings. A disease outbreak among people in the Four Corners area in 1993 led to the discovery of a new hantavirus strain, the Sin Nombre virus, and to the naming of a new disease, Hantavirus Pulmonary Syndrome, or HPS. Deer mice (*Peromyscus maniculatus*) are the main reservoir for the virus in the Southwest, but other rodents are known to carry it, too.

Infected rodents shed the Sin Nombre virus in their urine and feces. People typically get HPS when they inhale microscopic airborne particles or droplets (**aerosols**) produced directly by the animals or when contaminated dust and debris is stirred up. People may also be infected when contaminated materials come into contact with eyes or broken skin, or, possibly, by eating or drinking contaminated food or water. People have been infected with other hantaviruses by rodent bites, but this hasn't been proven to happen with the Sin Nombre virus.

The Sin Nombre virus isn't transmitted to people by ticks or biting insects, nor are there any known cases of transmission from one person to another.

The first symptoms of HPS typically appear about two weeks after exposure. They may include fever, severe muscle aches, cough, headache, and nausea. After a few days fluid builds up rapidly in the lungs, causing severe breathing difficulty, and intensive care treatment often becomes necessary. About half of all cases of HPS are fatal.

Anyone with rapidly-developing and severe shortness of breath should see a physician immediately. The sooner treatment begins, the better the chances of recovery.

Fortunately, cases of HPS are fairly rare; the disease doesn't seem easy to contract. Nevertheless, since the consequences of infection are potentially so serious, it's prudent to take precautions. Since there's no vaccine against hantavirus, the best way to prevent HPS is to avoid contact with wild rodents and their droppings, and, especially, to *avoid situations where you might breathe in virus-bearing aerosols.* See below.

Keeping wild rodents out of your house

The key is not to supply them with food, places to live, or entryways.

• Keep food (including pet food) in rodent-proof containers.

• Keep indoor garbage in tightly covered containers.

• Wash dishes immediately after use and clean up all spilled food.

• Get rid of indoor trash and clutter.

• Seal up or screen off all openings into the house a quarter-inch in diameter or larger.

• Place metal roof flashing around the base of a wooden or adobe dwelling up to a height of twelve inches and buried to a depth of six inches.

• Remove clutter and outdoor food sources (including pet food in feeding dishes) near the house.

Eliminating a rodent infestation

You can safely deal with minor rodent problems yourself by following the directions below. *However, a severe infestation, or a situation in which an occupant of the building has previously contracted HPS, requires special training, procedures, and equipment.* In such a case, don't proceed alone. Call your local or state health department for advice.

• Before working in a closed building or an enclosed area, ventilate it by opening doors and windows for thirty minutes. Use an exhaust fan if possible, and leave the area until the airing out is finished.

• Treat the infested area with an insecticide labeled for flea control, following the instructions on the label. (Fleas don't carry hantavirus but they do sometimes carry plague. They'll be looking for new hosts when the rodents are gone, and you'll be a candidate.)

• Set rodent snap-traps, using peanut butter for bait. (Traps are a better choice than poisons, which can harm non-target animals, people included.)

• Wear rubber gloves when removing dead rodents from snap traps. Follow the instructions under "clean-up," below, in disposing of the carcasses and disinfecting the gloves before taking them off.

• It's ok to use a live trap for a packrat so you can relocate it (see Question 28) but wear gloves when handling the trap,

and be careful not to get bitten. Disinfect the gloves and wash your hands afterward.

• Disinfect any snap trap or live trap that's no longer in use. Use one of the disinfectants described under "clean-up," below.

• Prevent a reinfestation by eliminating food sources, living places, and entryways.

Clean-up

The most important consideration is to *avoid any actions which might cause you to breathe in virus-carrying aerosols.* This is the main reason for using the wet-cleaning methods listed below. Before beginning, be sure you've ventilated the area and applied insecticide as described earlier. *Do not sweep or vacuum dry surfaces.*

• Wear rubber gloves.

• Thoroughly soak rodent carcasses, nests, and other contaminated debris with disinfectant before removal. Use a general-purpose disinfectant like Lysol®, or a bleach solution (one part bleach to ten parts water).

• Clean up debris using rags or paper towels, or a shovel for large accumulations like packrat houses.

• Place the wet materials in a plastic bag, seal the bag, then seal it in a second bag for extra safety. Then put the double-bagged materials in the trash. (In rural areas it's ok to bury the bags—but make sure they're at least two feet deep, to prevent animals from digging them up.)

• Mop floors or wipe countertops and other surfaces with a solution of water, detergent, and disinfectant.

• Rugs, carpets, and upholstered furniture can be normally steam-cleaned or shampooed. Contaminated laundry should be handled with rubber gloves and washed in hot water.

• Before removing your gloves, wash them in household disinfectant or bleach (1:10 dilution). After taking off the gloves, wash your hands with soap and water.

Hiking and camping

The chances of getting HPS during ordinary outdoor activities are extremely slim, but it makes sense to take some simple precautions.

• Avoid contact with rodents or their feces, burrows, or dens (including packrat houses).

• Don't pitch tents or place sleeping bags near rodent feces, burrows, or possible den sites.

• If possible, use a tent with a floor or sleep on a cot.

• Don't enter cabins or other shelters that are rodent infested.

• Keep food in rodent-proof containers, and don't leave garbage accessible to rodents.

• Make sure your water source is pure or the water has been disinfected.

Appendix E: HEAT-RELATED ILLNESS

This appendix describes symptoms and care for persons suffering from heat-related medical conditions. It was written in collaboration with Cynthia J. Anderson, Health and Safety Service Instructor Trainer, Central Arizona Chapter, American Red Cross.

The human body comes equipped with ways to deal with heat. When the body's temperature rises, it tries to shed heat through the skin. Blood vessels near the skin dilate (widen) to bring more warm blood to the surface, often causing the skin to visibly redden. The skin is also cooled by evaporation of sweat. When the air temperature is very warm, blood vessel dilation alone is less effective, and sweating increases.

When we exceed the body's natural ability to cope with heat, illness results. In more humid climates, heavy sweating is often the first sign the body is having trouble. However, in the dry desert air perspiration may evaporate so quickly that the skin remains dry, robbing of us our most obvious sign of impending heat-related illness. We must therefore pay extra attention to more subtle clues, such as thirst, tiredness, headache, and just feeling very hot.

Remember that heat emergencies can also exacerbate existing health problems, some of which may have gone undetected beforehand, and which may require additional care.

Heat can be stressful by itself, but high humidity increases its effects by interfering with perspiration. In the Sonoran Desert heat and high humidity are most likely to occur together during the summer monsoon. (See Question 2: Why is the Sonoran Desert so hot and dry? and Question 3: Are there seasons in the Sonoran Desert?)

Hot winds, which can occur at any time of year, can worsen the effects of heat by speeding dehydration, especially if we expose large areas of skin to the wind.

Other factors, such as type of clothing, how frequently we take breaks from exposure to high temperatures, how often, how much, and what kinds of fluids we drink, our physical condition, and the intensity of our activity can all affect how well our bodies manage high temperatures.

People at greatest risk for heat-related illness include:

• Those who work or exercise strenuously outdoors or in poorly cooled indoor areas.

• Elderly people.

• Young children.

• Those with health problems.

• Those who've had a heat-related illness in the past.

• Those who have respiratory or cardiovascular disease or other conditions that cause poor circulation.

• Those who routinely drink caffeinated beverages such as coffee, tea, and certain soft drinks. (Caffeine is a diuretic; it dehydrates the body by increasing urination.)

• Those who take diuretic medications.

People in good health can usually avoid heat-related illness during ordinary outdoor activities by using common sense, dressing appropriately, drinking enough, and minimizing exertion when it's hot. (See Question 31: What precautions should I take when hiking in the desert?)

Nevertheless, it's important for desert dwellers to be familiar with the signs and symptoms of heat-related conditions. When these occur, immediate care is called for. It's important to remember that heat-related illness is progressive: it tends to worsen unless the victim escapes the conditions that led to it, and it can become life-threatening.

Be sure to ask permission from the victim before giving aid in a heat emergency. If possible, get permission from a parent or guardian before aiding a child.

The three heat-related conditions described below, heat cramps, heat exhaustion, and heat stroke, are listed in order of increasing severity. However, they don't always develop in sequence.

HEAT CRAMPS

Heat cramps are painful spasms of skeletal muscles. The exact cause isn't known, but it's believed to be a combination of moisture loss and salt loss caused by heavy sweating. Heat cramps develop fairly rapidly and usually occur after unaccustomed exercise or work outdoors in warm or even moderate temperatures. However, heat cramps can also develop after prolonged exposure to heat without heavy exercise. They can even result from wearing overly heavy clothing in warm weather.

Although heat cramps are the least dangerous of the three heat-related conditions, they can indicate that a person is in the early stages of a more serious heat-related emergency.

Signs and symptoms

• Severe muscle contractions, usually in the legs and the abdomen, but they can occur in other muscles, also.

• Body temperature is usually normal and the skin is moist.

What to do

Usually, rest and fluids are all the body needs to recover.

• Have the victim rest comfortably in a cool place.

• Provide cool water or a commercial sports drink—half a glass (4 ounces) every 15 minutes for an hour. Avoid heavily sugared drinks.

• Lightly stretch the muscle and gently massage the area.

The victim should *not* take salt tablets or salt water. Swallowing high concentrations of salt can increase the likelihood of onset of heat exhaustion or heat stroke.

Once the cramps stop and there's no other evidence of illness, the person can usually resume activity, but caution him or her to be aware of signs and symptoms of developing heat exhaustion or heat stroke. Advise the victim to drink plenty of the appropriate fluids whenever exposed to hot conditions, and especially during or after activity.

HEAT EXHAUSTION

Heat exhaustion typically occurs after long periods of strenuous exercise or work in a hot environment. However, the condition can also develop after prolonged exposure to heat even without strenuous exercise. Over time, the victim loses fluid through sweating, which decreases the blood volume. As blood flow to the skin increases, flow to the vital organs is reduced, and the person goes into mild shock.

Heat exhaustion is an early indication that the body's temperature regulating mechanism is becoming overwhelmed. Heat exhaustion isn't always preceded by heat cramps.

Signs and symptoms.

• Normal or below normal body temperature.

• Cool, moist, pale skin. (But skin may be red in an early stage, immediately following exertion.)

• Headache.

• Nausea.

• Dizziness and weakness.

• Exhaustion.

What to do

• Cool the body by any means available. Move the victim out of the sun or into a cool indoor area if possible. Loosen or remove tight or heavy clothing. Apply cool, wet cloths to the skin. Fan the victim. Cold packs or ice may be applied to the wrists, ankles, armpits, or neck to cool major blood vessels. (*Do not* apply rubbing alcohol. It closes the pores and prevents heat loss.)

• Give water. If the victim is conscious, have him or her drink cool water (not ice water) slowly. (The victim is likely to be nauseated and water is less likely than other fluids to cause vomiting.) Don't let the victim drink too quickly; give a half glass (4 oz) every 15 minutes for an hour.

• Let the victim rest in a comfortable position, and watch carefully for changes in his or her condition. Caution the victim not to resume normal activities the same day.

Often the victim will feel better after resting in a cool place and drinking water. However, if heat exhaustion is allowed to progress it can advance to life-threatening heat stroke. Refusing water, vomiting, and changing levels of consciousness are all signs that the victim's condition is worsening. If any of these occur, get medical assistance. Dial 911.

HEAT STROKE

Heat stroke is the least common and most severe heat-related illness. It most often occurs when people ignore the signs and symptoms of heat exhaustion. However, a victim can develop heat stroke with no noticeable prior symptoms of heat exhaustion.

Heat stroke develops when the body systems are overwhelmed by heat and begin to stop functioning. Sweating stops because body fluid levels are low. Without perspiration the body can't cool itself effectively, and body temperature rapidly rises. It soon reaches a level at which the brain and other vital organs begin to fail.

Heat stroke is a life-threatening medical emergency, and the immediate threat is the body's high temperature, not lack of water. It's essential to cool the body right away; giving water can come later.

Signs and symptoms

• High body temperature (often as high as 106°F).

• Red, hot, dry skin.

• Progressive loss of consciousness.

• Rapid, weak pulse. (May become weak and irregular if the victim's condition deteriorates.)

• Rapid, shallow breathing.

What to do

• Get emergency medical help. Dial 911.

• *Cool the body as quickly as possible* as described under heat exhaustion, above. Don't shock the victim by (for example) pouring ice water over him or her.

• Once the body has been cooled, give water if the victim is conscious, and keep him or her comfortable, again as described under heat exhaustion, above.

• In advanced or prolonged cases, trained personnel may need to administer rescue breathing ("artificial respiration") or CPR (cardio-pulmonary resuscitation).

Appendix F: PRONUNCIATION GUIDE TO NON-ENGLISH TERMS

This appendix gives pronunciations of some non-English words commonly encountered in the Sonoran Desert north of Mexico. Most of the words are Spanish or derived from Native American languages.

Pronunciations of Spanish words are often anglicized to varying degrees, depending on the speaker. The pronunciations given here are close to the original Spanish. Where a markedly different anglicized form is often heard, it's listed in parentheses.

Incidentally, "Joshua," as in "Joshua tree," is an English name, spoken with an opening j sound (not an h sound, as in Spanish).

A

Agave: *ah-GAH-vay*

Agua caliente: *AHG-wah* or *AH-wah cal-YEN-tay*

Ajo: *AH-ho*

Algodones: *ahl-go-DOH-nays*

Ak chin: *ahk cheen*

B

Baboquivari: *bah-bo-KEE-va-ree*

Baja: *BAH-ha*

Bajada: *bah-HAH-dah*

Borrego: *bo-RAY-go*

Buenos Aires: *BWAY-nos EYE-rays*

C

Cabeza Prieta: *cah-Bay-sah pree-AY-tah*

Cahuilla: *kah-WEE-yah*

Caliche: *kah-LEE-chay* (more often: *kuh-LEE-chee*)

Caracara: *KAH-ruh-cah-ruh*

Casa Grande: *KAH-sah GRAHN-day* (often, for the city: *KA-suh grand*)

Chaparral: *cha-pah-RAHL* (*sha-puh-RAL*)

Cholla: *CHOY-yah*

Chihuahua: *chee-WAH-wah*

Chiricahua: *chee-ree-CAH-wah*

Chubasco: *choo-BOS-co*

Chulo: *CHOO-lo*

Chuparosa: *choo-pah-RO-sah*

Ciénega: *see-AY-neg-ah*

Coati: *ko-AH-tee*

Coatimundi: *ko-ah-tee-MOON-dee* (*ko-a-ti-MUN-dee*)

Coyote: *ko-YO-tay* (*ky-O-tee, KY-ote*)

E

Estrella: *es-TRAY-yah*

G

Galiuro: *gah-lee-UR-o* (*guh-LUR-o*)

Gila: *HEE-lah*

H

Harcuvar: *HAR-koo-vahr*

Harquahala: *HAR-kwa-hah-lah* (*HAR-kwa-hay-luh*)

Hohokam: *ho-ho-KAHM*

Huachuca: *wah-CHOO-kah*

Hualapai: *WAH-lah-pie*

J

Javelina: *hah-vah-LEE-nah*

Jojoba: *ho-HO-bah*

M

Madre: *MAH-dray*

Manzanita: *mahn-sah-NEE-tah*
   (*man-zuh-NEE-tuh*)

Maricopa: *mah-ree-CO-pah*

Mariposa: *mah-ree-PO-sa*

Mazatzal: *mah-saht-SAHL*

Mesa: *MAY-sah*

Mohave or Mojave: *mo-HAH-vay*

N

Nogales: *no-GAH-lays*

Nolina: *no-LEE-nah*

O

Ocotillo: *o-co-TEE-yo*

P

Paloverde: *pah-lo-VAIR-day*
   (*pa-lo-VER-dee*)

Phainopepla: *fay-no-PEP-luh*

Picacho: *pee-CAH-cho*

Pima: *PEE-mah*

Pinal: *pee-NAHL*

Pinacate: *pee-nah-CAH-tay*

Pinaleño: *pee-nah-LAY-neeo*
   (*pee-nuh-LAY-no*)

Playa: *PLY-yuh*

Puma: *POO-mah*
   (*PEEOO-muh*)

Pyrrhuloxia: *pir-uh-LOK-see-uh*

S

Saguaro: *sah-WAR-o*

San Jacinto: *sahn hah-SEEN-toh*

San Xavier: *sahn ha-VEER*

Sonora: *so-NO-rah*

Sotol: *SO-tol*

T

Tinaja: *tee-NAH-hah*

Tohono O'odham: *to-HO-no o-O-dahm*
   (pronounce o as in "short")

Tortolita: *tor-toh-LEE-tah*

Tucson: *TOO-sahn*

V

Virga: *VUR-guh*

Y

Yaqui: *YAH-kee*

Yavapai: *YAH-vah-pie*

Yucca: *YUK-ah*

Appendix G: ADDITIONAL SOURCES

This appendix will help you locate sources of further information related to the forty-two questions in the *Arizona-Sonora Desert Museum Book of Answers*. See the Bibliography and Organizations list following this appendix to find the books and organizations indicated by the numbers.

References are given separately for several sidebars that differ markedly in subject matter from the questions.

SECTION ONE:
GETTING TO KNOW THE DESERT

Q1 What exactly is a desert?
Bibliography: 3-6 8 9 60 103 166 177 198
Organizations: 28 30 35 39 41 45 46

Q2 Why is the Sonoran Desert so hot and dry?
Bibliography: 3-6 8-10 60 103 150 166 197 198
Organizations: 28-30 35 39 41 45 46

Q3 Are there seasons in the Sonoran Desert?
Bibliography: 7 14 15 19 20 46 192 194 199
Organizations: 28 30 35 39 41 45 46

Q4 Why are sunsets so spectacular in the Sonoran Desert?
Bibliography: 149-153
Organizations: 28 30 41 46

Q5 How can I tell cacti from other spiny desert plants?
Bibliography: 28 42 45 47 48 50-52 54 56 60 63 194
Organizations: 1 2 28-30 35 36 39 41 42 45 46

Q6 Which Sonoran Desert plants are most often mistaken for cacti?
Bibliography: 11 43 45 47 63
Organizations: 1 2 28-30 35 36 39 41 42 45 46

Q7 How old do desert plants get?
Bibliography: 40 195 200
Organizations: 28-30 35 39 41 42 44-46

For "Queen Clone?" sidebar
Bibliography: 11 14 194
Organizations: 28 30 35 39 42 44-46

Q8 Are saguaros endangered?
Bibliography: 5 15 17 37 38 189 193 194
Organizations: 28-30 35 36 41

Q9 What are the frogs I hear at night during the summer rains?
Bibliography: 5 6 8 9 11 20 30 36 66 76 90 93 103 113 194
Organizations: 5 7-10 28 35 39 41 45 46

Q10 Is a javelina a pig?
Bibliography: 14 15 29 35 68 70 77 84 102 126 194
Organizations: 28 35 41 50 52 53

Q11 How do Sonoran Desert cities get their water?
Bibliography: 5 140-148 195 199
Organizations: 12 28-30 35 41 44-46 69 70 72-81

Q12 How did Indians live in the
     Sonoran Desert?
     Bibliography: 1 5 21-23 136-139
     142 191
     Organizations: 26 27 30-35 37-39
     41 45 46

SECTION TWO:
AROUND THE HOME

Q13 Do I need to water native desert
     plants?
     Bibliography: 10 103 117-119 122
     127 130
     Organizations: 28-30 35 36 39 41
     42 45 46 67-76 78-80

     For "Life on the Dry Side" sidebar
     Bibliography: 4-6 8 9 11 46 166
     194 198
     Organizations: 1 2 28-30 35 39 41
     42 44-46

Q14 How should I transplant cacti?
     Bibliography: 117 127
     Organizations: 28-30 35 36 41 42
     46 65-68

Q15 What's the concrete-like stuff buried
     in my garden?
     Bibliography: 127 198
     Organizations: 28-30 35 36 41 42
     45 46 67 68

Q16 How can I keep wild animals from
     eating the plants in my garden?
     Bibliography: 120 126
     Organizations: 28-30 35 36 41 42
     46 52 53 67 68

Q17 How can I attract desert wildlife to
     my yard?
     Bibliography: 117 120 123 124 126
     135
     Organizations: 28-30 35 36 39 41
     42 45 46 52 53 67 68

For "Butterfly Gardening" sidebar
Bibliography: 115 116 123 125 129
132 133
Organizations: 1-4 28-30 35 36 39
41 42 45 46

Q18 How can I attract hummingbirds?
     Bibliography: 11 25 29 32 34 39
     116 117 120 123 128 131 134
     135
     Organizations: 11 28-30 35 36 39
     41 42 45 46

Q19 Don't birds sometimes catch a
     disease at feeders and birdbaths?
     Bibliography: 117
     Organizations: 11 35 39 41 45 46
     50 52 53

Q20 What should I do about an injured,
     sick, or orphaned animal in my
     yard?
     Bibliography: 120
     Organizations: 11 28 35 39 41 45
     46 52 53 67 68

Q21 How should I identify bark
     scorpions, black widows, and
     brown spiders?
     Bibliography: 6 11 24 79 81 83 101
     106 107 110 111 113
     Organizations: 3 4 28 29 35 39 41
     45 46 67 68

Q22 How can I keep dangerous
     scorpions and spiders out of
     my house?
     Bibliography: 24 101 111 113
     Organizations: 3 4 28 39 41 46
     67 68

Q23 How can I tell if the bees in my
     yard are Africanized?
     Bibliography: 101 109 114 189
     Organizations: 3 4 28 41 45 46
     67 68

Q24 How dangerous are Africanized bees?
Bibliography: 101 109 113 114 189
Organizations: 3 4 28 41 45 46 67 68

Q25 What kind of snake is in my yard?
Bibliography: 66 76 83 91 93 103
Organizations: 5 7-10 28 39 41 44-46 67 68

Q26 How can I keep rattlesnakes out of my yard?
Bibliography: 6 31 78 111 113 120
Organizations: 5 7-10 28 39 41 46 52 53

For "A Gila Monster in Every Garage" sidebar
Bibliography: 5 11 66 76 91 93 111 112
Organizations: 5 7-10 28 39 41 44-46

Q27 How can I stop woodpeckers from making holes in my house?
Bibliography: 120
Organizations: 11 28 39 41 46 52 53 67 68

Q28 Why do packrats keep making houses in my car's engine compartment?
Bibliography: 5 6 8 11 29 84 101 111 113 190
Organizations: 3 4 28 39 41 45 46 52 53 67 68 84-98 100

For "Packrats and Paleoecologists" sidebar
Bibliography: 4 188
Organizations: 28 39 41 44-46

Q29 How can I protect my pets from coyotes and bobcats?
Bibliography: 11 26 29 78 84 120
Organizations: 28 39 41 46 52 53

SECTION THREE:
ENJOYING THE OUTDOORS

Q30 What might I bring on a hike to help me enjoy the desert?
Bibliography: 6 103 156 163 165 166 173 194
Organizations: 21 28 39 41 45 46

Q31 What precautions should I take when hiking in the desert?
Bibliography: 5 6 8 33 103 156 163 165 166 173 190
Organizations: 21 28 35 39 41 44 46

Q32 If I run out of water in the desert can I get some from a barrel cactus?
Bibliography: 5 6 196
Organizations: 28 30 35 39 41 45 46

For "Teetotalers" sidebar
Bibliography: 1 8 11 13 29 33
Organizations: 28 41 44-46

Q33 Are cactus spines poisonous?
Bibliography: 1 5 6 8 14 194
Organizations: 1 2 28-30 35 36 39 41 42 45 46

Q34 Why don't I see very many animals when I hike in the desert?
Bibliography: 7 30 161 162 171 184 185 194
Organizations: 3 4-11 28 35 39 41 45 46 52 53

Q35 How dangerous are Sonoran Desert toads?
Bibliography: 19 76 110 113
Organizations: 5 7-10 28 41 52

Q36 If I find a desert tortoise would it be all right to take it home as a pet?
Bibliography: 11 14 29 76

Organizations: 5-10 28 35 39 41
44-46 50 52 53

Q37 How can I avoid dangerous
encounters with rattlers and
Gila monsters?
Bibliography: 5 6 8 11 14 15 19 30
31 78 105 108 110-113 173 194
Organizations: 5 7-10 28 35 39 41
45 46 52 53

Q38 Are there other venomous reptiles in
the Sonoran Desert?
Bibliography: 6 11 66 91 93 103
108 110-113 194
Organizations: 5 7-10 28 35 39 41
44 46 52 53

Q39 What is valley fever?
Bibliography: (none)
Organizations: 35 41 45 46 84-98
101

Q40 What precautions should I take
when driving in the desert?
Bibliography: 6 8 159 166
Organizations: 35 39 41 46

Q41 How can I minimize my impact on
the desert?
Bibliography: 6 8 156 159 169 194
Organizations: 21 28 30 35 39 41
44-46 48-53

For "The Desert's Upper Crust"
sidebar
Bibliography: 11
Organizations: 28 30 39 46

Q42 What else can I do to explore the
desert?
Bibliography: 154-164 166-168
170-187 192 194
Organizations: 1-64

BIBLIOGRAPHY

Most of the books listed here are available in bookstores, but a few especially interesting out-of-print titles are included. These older publications are available in public libraries.

To find out which books have information related to a specific question in the *Arizona-Sonora Desert Museum Book of Answers*, see Appendix G: Additional Sources. The books are numbered for reference in that appendix.

INTRODUCTION TO THE DESERT AND DESERT PLACES

1 Broyles, Bill. *Organ Pipe Cactus National Monument*. Tucson: Southwest Parks and Monuments Association, 1996.

2 Evans, Doris. *Saguaro National Monument*. Tucson: Southwest Parks and Monuments Association, 1993.

3 Hanson, Roseann Beggy, and Jonathan Hanson. *Discovering the Desert Museum and the Sonoran Desert Region*. Tucson: Arizona-Sonora Desert Museum Press, 1996.

4 Helms, Christopher L. *Sonoran Desert: The Story Behind the Scenery*. Las Vegas, NV: KC Publications, 1980.

5 Kirk, Ruth. Desert: *The American Southwest*. Boston: Houghton Mifflin Co., 1973.

6 Larson, Peggy. *A Sierra Club Naturalist's Guide to the Deserts of the Southwest*. San Francisco: Sierra Club Books, 1977.

7 Lazaroff, David Wentworth. *Sabino Canyon: The Life of a Southwestern Oasis*. Tucson: University of Arizona Press, 1993.

8 Olin, George. *House in the Sun: A Natural History of the Sonoran Desert*. Tucson: Southwest Parks and Monuments Association, 1994.

9 Page, Jake. *Arid Lands*. Alexandria, VA: Time-Life Books, 1984. (Planet Earth series)

10 Schad, Jerry. *California Deserts*. Helena, MT: Falcon Press Publishing Company, 1997.

11 Tweit, Susan J. *The Great Southwest Nature Factbook*. Anchorage: Alaska Northwest Books, 1992.

12 Van Dyke, John C. *The Desert*. Tucson: Arizona Historical Society, 1976. (Reprint of the 1903 second edition.)

13 Zwinger, Ann Haymond. *The Mysterious Lands: A Naturalist Explores the Four Great Deserts of the Southwest*. New York: Truman Talley Books/Plume, 1989.

ESSAYS ON NATURE AND CULTURE

14 Alcock, John. *Sonoran Desert Spring*. Tucson: University of Arizona Press, 1994.

15 Alcock, John. *Sonoran Desert Summer*. Tucson: University of Arizona Press, 1990.

16 Bowden, Charles. *The Sonoran Desert*. New York: Harry N. Abrams, Inc., 1992.

17 Bowers, Janice Emily. *Fear Falls Away and Other Essays from Hard and Rocky Places*. Tucson: University of Arizona Press, 1997.

18 Bowers, Janice Emily. *The Mountains Next Door*. Tucson: University of Arizona Press, 1991.

19 Cowles, Raymond B., and Elna S. Bakker. *Desert Journal: Reflections of a Naturalist*. Berkeley: University of California Press, 1977.

20 Krutch, Joseph Wood. *The Desert Year*. Tucson: University of Arizona Press, 1985. (First published 1952.)

21 Nabhan, Gary Paul. *Cultures of Habitat: On Nature, Culture, and Story*. Washington, D.C.: Counterpoint, 1997.

22 Nabhan, Gary Paul. *The Desert Smells Like Rain: A Naturalist in Papago Country*. San Francisco: North Point Press, 1982.

23 Nabhan, Gary Paul. *Gathering the Desert*. Tucson: University of Arizona Press, 1985.

PLANTS AND ANIMALS— DESCRIPTION

24 Friederici, Peter. *Strangers in our Midst: The Startling World of Sonoran Desert Arthropods*. Tucson: Arizona-Sonora Desert Museum Press, 1997.

25 Greenewalt, Crawford H. *Hummingbirds*. New York: Dover Publications, 1990. (First published 1960.)

26 Hanson, Jonathan, and Roseann Beggy Hanson. *Desert Dogs: Coyotes, Foxes, and Wolves*. Tucson: Arizona-Sonora Desert Museum Press, 1996.

27 Hodge, Carle. *All About Saguaros*. Phoenix: Arizona Highways, 1991.

28 Houk, Rose. *Wild Cactus*. New York: Artisan, 1996.

29 Jaeger, Edmund C. *Desert Wildlife*. Stanford: Stanford University Press, 1961.

30 Kappel-Smith, Diana. *Night Life: Nature from Dusk to Dawn*. Tucson: University of Arizona Press, 1990.

31 Klauber, Laurence. *Rattlesnakes: Their Habits, Life Histories, and Influence on Mankind*. Berkeley: University of California Press, 1982. (Abridged version of a work first published in 1956.)

32 Lazaroff, David Wentworth. *The Secret Lives of Hummingbirds*. Tucson: Arizona-Sonora Desert Museum Press, 1995.

33 Schmidt-Nielsen, Knut. *Desert Animals: Physiological Problems of Heat and Water*. New York: Dover Publications, 1979. (First published 1964.)

34 Skutch, Alexander F. *The Life of the Hummingbird*. New York: Crown Publishers, 1973.

35 Sowls, Lyle K. *The Peccaries*. Tucson: University of Arizona Press, 1984.

36 Stebbins, Robert C., and Nathan W. Cohen. *A Natural History of Amphibians*. Princeton, NJ: Princeton University Press, 1995.

37 Steenbergh, Warren F., and Charles H. Lowe. *Ecology of the Saguaro: II. Reproduction, Germination, Establishment, Growth, and Survival of the Young Plant*. National Park Service Scientific Monograph Series No. 8, 1977.

38 Steenbergh, Warren F., and Charles H. Lowe. *Ecology of the Saguaro: III. Growth and Demography*. National Park Service Scientific Monograph Series No. 17, 1983.

39 Toops, Connie. *Hummingbirds: Jewels in Flight*. Stillwater, MN: Voyageur Press, 1992.

40 Turner, Raymond M., Janice E. Bowers, and Tony L. Burgess. *Sonoran Desert Plants: An Ecological Atlas*. Tucson: University of Arizona Press, 1995.

PLANTS—IDENTIFICATION

41 Ayer, Eleanor H. *Arizona Wildflowers: A Guide to Common Species*. Frederick, CO: Renaissance House, 1989.

42 Benson, Lyman. *The Cacti of the United States and Canada*. Stanford: Stanford University Press, 1982.

43 Benson, Lyman, and Robert A. Darrow. *Trees and Shrubs of the Southwestern Deserts*. Tucson: University of Arizona Press, 1981.

44 Bowers, Janice Emily. *100 Desert Wildflowers of the Southwest*. Tucson: Southwest Parks and Monuments Association, 1989.

45 Bowers, Janice Emily. *Shrubs and Trees of the Southwest Deserts*. Tucson: Southwest Parks and Monuments Association, 1993.

46 Desert Botanical Garden staff. *Desert Wildflowers: A Guide to Identifying, Locating, and Enjoying Arizona Wildflowers and Cactus Blossoms*. Phoenix: Arizona Highways, 1988.

47 Dodge, Natt N. *Flowers of the Southwest Deserts*. Tucson: Southwest Parks and Monuments Association, 1985.

48 Earle, W. Hubert. Cacti of the Southwest. Tempe, AZ: Rancho Arroyo Book Distributor, 1980.

49 Epple, Anne Orth. *A Field Guide to the Plants of Arizona*. Helena, MT: Falcon Press Publishing Co., 1995.

50 Fischer, Pierre C. *70 Common Cacti of the Southwest*. Tucson: Southwest Parks and Monuments Association, 1989.

51 Heil, Kenneth D. *Familiar Cacti*. New York: Alfred A. Knopf, Inc., 1993. (Audubon Society Pocket Guide)

52 Hickman, James C., ed. *The Jepson Manual: Higher Plants of California*. Berkeley: University of California Press, 1993.

53 Jaeger, Edmund C. *Desert Wildflowers*. Stanford: Stanford University Press, 1969.

54 Kearney, Thomas H., and Robert H. Peebles. *Arizona Flora*. Second Edition with Supplement by John Thomas Howell and Elizabeth McClintock. Berkeley: University of California Press, 1960.

55 Leake, Dorothy VanDyke, John Benjamin Leake, and Marcelotte Leake Roeder. *Desert and Mountain Plants of the Southwest*. Norman: University of Oklahoma Press, 1993.

56 Munz, Philip A., and David D. Keck. *A California Flora and Supplement*. Berkeley: University of California Press, 1973.

57 Nelson, Richard and Sharon. *Easy Field Guide to Common Desert Cactus of Arizona*. Phoenix: Primer Publishers, 1996.

58 Niehaus, Theodore F. *A Field Guide to Southwestern and Texas Wildflowers*. Boston: Houghton Mifflin Co., 1984. (Peterson Field Guide Series)

59 Parker, Kittie F. *An Illustrated Guide to Arizona Weeds*. Tucson: University of Arizona Press, 1972.

60 Shreve, Forrest, and Ira L. Wiggins. *Vegetation and Flora of the Sonoran Desert*. Stanford: Stanford University Press, 1964.

61 Spellenberg, Richard. *National Audubon Society Field Guide to North American Wildflowers: Western Region*. New York: Alfred A. Knopf, Inc., 1994.

62 Tucson Citizen. *Southern Arizona Wild Flower Guide*. Tucson: Tucson Citizen, 1972.

63 Vines, Robert A. *Trees, Shrubs, and Woody Vines of the Southwest*. Austin: University of Texas Press, 1960.

64 Watts, Mary Theilgaard, and Tom Watts. *Desert Tree Finder: A Pocket Manual for Identifying Desert Trees*. Rochester, NY: Nature Study Guild, 1974.

ANIMALS—IDENTIFICATION

65 Bailowitz, Richard A., and James P. Brock. *Butterflies of Southeastern Arizona*. Tucson: Sonoran Arthropod Studies Institute, 1991.

66 Behler, John L. *National Audubon Society Field Guide to North American Reptiles and Amphibians*. New York: Alfred A. Knopf, Inc., 1997.

67 Borror, Donald J., and Richard E. White. *A Field Guide to the Insects*. Boston: Houghton Mifflin Co., 1970. (Peterson Field Guide Series)

68 Burt, William Henry, and Richard Philip Grossenheider. *A Field Guide to the Mammals: North America North of Mexico*. Boston: Houghton Mifflin Company, 1980. (Peterson Field Guide Series)

69 Cockrum, E. Lendell, and Yar Petryszyn. *Mammals of California and Nevada*. Tucson: Treasure Chest Publications, 1994.

70 Cockrum, E. Lendell, and Yar Petryszyn. *Mammals of the Southwestern United States and Northwestern Mexico*. Tucson: Treasure Chest Publications, 1992.

71 Cunningham, Richard L. *50 Common Birds of the Southwest*. Tucson: Southwest Parks and Monuments Association, 1990.

72 Davis, Barbara L. *A Field Guide to Birds of the Desert Southwest*. Houston: Gulf Publishing Company, 1997.

73 Farrand, John, Jr. *Western Birds*. New York: McGraw-Hill Book Co., 1988. (An Audubon Handbook)

74 Gray, Mary Taylor. *Watchable Birds of the Southwest*. Missoula, MT: Mountain Press Publishing Co., 1995.

75 Griggs, Jack L. *All the Birds of North America*. New York: Harper Collins Publishers, 1997. (American Bird Conservancy's Field Guide)

76 Hanson, Jonathan, and Roseann Beggy Hanson. *50 Common Reptiles and Amphibians of the Southwest*. Tucson: Southwest Parks and Monuments Association, 1997.

77 Hoffmeister, Donald F. *Mammals of Arizona*. Tucson: University of Arizona Press and Arizona Game and Fish Department, 1986.

78 Kopp, April. *Creatures, Critters and Crawlers of the Southwest*. Santa Fe: New Mexico Magazine, 1996.

79 Levi, Herbert W., and Lorna R. Levi. *Spiders and Their Kin*. New York: Golden Press, 1987. (A Golden Guide)

80 Miller, Millie, and Cyndi Nelson. *Hummers: Hummingbirds of North America*. Boulder, CO: Johnson Books, 1987.

81 Milne, Lorus and Margery. *National Audubon Society Field Guide to North American Insects and Spiders*. New York: Alfred A. Knopf, Inc., 1996.

82 Murie, Olaus J. *A Field Guide to Animal Tracks*. Boston: Houghton Mifflin Co., 1982. (Peterson Field Guide Series)

83 Nelson, Richard and Sharon. Easy Field Guide Series. Phoenix: Primer Publishers.
Common Desert Birds, 1995.
Common Desert Insects, 1995.
Common Desert Mammals of Arizona, 1985.
Southwestern Snakes, 1996.

84 Olin, George. *Mammals of the Southwest Deserts*. Tucson: Southwest Parks and Monuments Association, 1988. (Revised edition)

85 Peterson, Roger Tory. *A Field Guide to Western Birds*. Boston: Houghton Mifflin Co., 1990. (Peterson Field Guide Series)

86 Putnam, Patti and Milt. *North America's Favorite Butterflies: A Pictorial Guide*. Minocqua, WI: Willow Creek Press, 1997.

87 Pyle, Robert Michael. *National Audubon Society Field Guide to North American Butterflies*. New York: Alfred A. Knopf, Inc., 1995.

88 Robbins, Chandler S., Bertel Brunn, and Herbert S. Zim. *Birds of North America: A Field Guide to Bird Identification*. New York: Golden Press, 1983. (Golden Field Guide)

89 Scott, Shirley L, ed. *Field Guide to the Birds of North America*. Washington, D.C.: National Geographic Society, 1987.

90 Smith, Hobart M. *Amphibians of North America: A Guide to Field Identification*. New York: Golden Press, 1978. (Golden Field Guide)

91 Smith, Hobart M., and Edmund D. Brodie, Jr. *Reptiles of North America: A Guide to Field Identification*. New York: Golden Press, 1982. (Golden Field Guide)

92 Stall, Chris. *Animal Tracks of the Southwest States: Arizona, New Mexico, Southern Nevada, Southern Utah, and Southwest Colorado*. Seattle: The Mountaineers, 1990.

93 Stebbins, Robert C. *A Field Guide to Western Reptiles and Amphibians*. Boston: Houghton Mifflin Co., 1985. (Peterson Field Guide Series)

94 Stokes, Donald and Lillian. *Stokes Beginner's Guide to Birds: Western Region*. Boston: Little, Brown and Co., 1996.

95 Stokes, Donald and Lillian. *Stokes Field Guide to the Birds: Western Region.* Boston: Little, Brown and Co., 1996.

96 Sutton, Clay, and Richard K. Walton. *North American Birds of Prey.* New York: Alfred A. Knopf, Inc. 1994. (National Audubon Society Pocket Guide)

97 Tilden, James W., and Arthur C. Smith. *A Field Guide to Western Butterflies.* Boston, Houghton Mifflin Co., 1986. (Peterson Field Guide Series)

98 Uvardy, Miklos D. F. *National Audubon Society Field Guide to North American Birds: Western Region.* New York: Alfred A. Knopf, Inc. 1995.

99 Walton, Richard K. *Familiar Butterflies of North America.* New York: Alfred A. Knopf, Inc., 1995.

100 Walton, Richard K. *Songbirds and Familiar Backyard Birds: West.* New York: Alfred A. Knopf, Inc., 1994. (National Audubon Society Pocket Guide)

101 Werner, Floyd, and Carl Olson. *Insects of the Southwest: How to Identify Helpful, Harmful, and Venomous Insects.* Tucson: Fisher Books, 1994.

102 Whitaker, John O., Jr. *National Audubon Society Field Guide to North American Mammals.* New York: Alfred A. Knopf, Inc., 1997.

PLANTS AND ANIMALS— IDENTIFICATION

103 MacMahon, James A. *Deserts.* New York: Alfred A. Knopf, Inc., 1985. (Audubon Society Nature Guide)

104 Miller, Millie, and Cyndi Nelson. *Desert Critters: Plants and Animals of the Southwest.* Boulder, CO: Johnson Books, 1996.

VENOMOUS ANIMALS

105 Brown, David E., and Neil B. Carmony. *Gila Monster: Facts and Folklore of America's Aztec Lizard.* Silver City, NM: High-Lonesome Books, 1991.

106 Cornett, James W. *The Black Widow: Answers to Frequently Asked Questions.* Palm Springs: Palm Springs Desert Museum, 1994.

107 Cornett, James W. *Scorpions!: Answers to Frequently Asked Questions.* Palm Springs: Palm Springs Desert Museum, 1993.

108 Ernst, Carl H. *Venomous Reptiles of North America.* Washington, D.C.: Smithsonian Institution Press, 1992.

109 Flakus, Greg. *Living with Killer Bees: The Story of the Africanized Bee Invasion.* Oakland, CA: Quick Trading Company, 1993.

110 Foster, Steven, and Roger Caras. *A Field Guide to Venomous Animals and Poisonous Plants.* Boston: Houghton Mifflin Co., 1994. (Peterson Field Guide Series)

111 Hare, Trevor. *Poisonous Dwellers of the Desert.* Tucson: Southwest Parks and Monuments Association, 1995. (Revised edition)

112 Lowe, Charles H., Cecil R. Schwalbe, and Terry B. Johnson. *The Venomous Reptiles of Arizona.* Phoenix: Arizona Game and Fish Department, 1986.

113 Smith, Robert L. *Venomous Animals of Arizona*. Tucson: University of Arizona College of Agriculture Cooperative Extension Service Bulletin 8245, 1982.

114 Winston, Mark L. Killer Bees: *The Africanized Honey Bee in the Americas*. Cambridge: Harvard University Press, 1992.

HOUSE AND GARDEN

115 Alcock, John. *In a Desert Garden: Love and Death Among the Insects*. New York: W. W. Norton and Co., 1997.

116 Arbuckle, Nancy, and Cedric Crocker. *How to Attract Hummingbirds and Butterflies*. San Ramon, CA: Ortho Books, 1991.

117 Arizona Native Plant Society Urban Landscape Committee. Desert landscaping series. Tucson: Arizona Native Plant Society.
Desert Accent Plants, 1992.
Desert Bird Gardening, 1997.
Desert Butterfly Gardening, 1996.
(With Sonoran Arthropod Studies Institute)
Desert Grasses, 1993.
Desert Ground Covers and Vines, 1991.
Desert Shrubs, 1990.
Desert Trees, 1990.
Desert Wildflowers, 1991.

118 Brenzel, Kathleen Norris, ed. *Sunset Western Garden Book*. Menlo Park, CA: Sunset Publishing Corporation, 1995.

119 Brown-Folsom, Debra, John N. Trager, James Folsom, Joe Clementz, and Nancy Scott. *Dry Climate Gardening with Succulents*. New York: Pantheon Books, 1995.

120 California Center for Wildlife. *Living with Wildlife: How to Enjoy, Cope with, and Protect North America's Wild Creatures Around Your Home and Theirs*. San Francisco: Sierra Club Books, 1994.

121 Denver Water. *Xeriscape Plant Guide: 100 Water-Wise Plants for Gardens and Landscapes*. Golden, CO: Fulcrum Publishing, 1996.

122 Duffield, Mary Rose, and Warren D. Jones. *Plants for Dry Climates: How to Select, Grow and Enjoy*. Los Angeles: HP Books, 1992.

123 Ellis, Barbara. *Attracting Birds and Butterflies: How to Plan and Plant a Backyard Habitat*. Boston: Houghton Mifflin Company, 1997.

124 Engel-Wilson, Carolyn. *Landscaping for Desert Wildlife*. Phoenix: Arizona Game and Fish Department, 1992.

125 Gunnarson, Linda, and Frances Haselsteiner. *Butterfly Gardening*. San Francisco: Sierra Club Books, 1990.

126 Hoffa, Robert L. *Coexisting with Urban Wildlife: A Guide to the Central Arizona Uplands*. Prescott, AZ: Sharlot Hall Museum Press, 1996.

127 Mielke, Judy. Native *Plants for Southwestern Landscapes*. Austin: University of Texas Press, 1993.

128 Newfield, Nancy L., and Barbara Nielsen. *Hummingbird Gardens: Attracting Nature's Jewels to Your Backyard*. Shelburne, VT: Chapters Publishing Ltd., 1996.

129 Schneck, Marcus. *Creating a Butterfly Garden: A Guide to Attracting and Identifying Butterfly Visitors*. New York: Simon and Schuster, Inc., 1993.

130 Shuler, Carol. *Low-Water-Use Plants for California and the Southwest*. Tucson: Fisher Books, 1993.

131 Stokes, Donald and Lillian. *The Hummingbird Book: The Complete Guide to Attracting, Identifying, and Enjoying Hummingbirds*. Boston: Little, Brown, and Co., 1989.

132 Stokes, Donald and Lillian, and Ernest Williams. *The Butterfly Book: An Easy Guide to Butterfly Gardening, Identification, and Behavior*. Boston: Little, Brown and Co., 1991.

133 Tekulsky, Mathew. *The Butterfly Garden: Turning Your Garden, Window Box or Backyard into a Beautiful Home for Butterflies*. Harvard: The Harvard Common Press, 1985.

134 Tekulsky, Mathew. *The Hummingbird Garden: Turning Your Garden, Window Box, or Backyard into a Beautiful Home for Hummingbirds*. Harvard: The Harvard Common Press, 1990.

135 Wasowski, Sally and Andy. *Native Gardens for Dry Climates*. New York: Clarkson Potter/Publishers, 1995.

NATIVE AMERICANS

136 Fontana, Bernard L. *Of Earth and Little Rain: The Papago Indians*. Flagstaff, AZ: Northland Press, 1989.

137 Sheridan, Thomas E., and Nancy J. Parezo. *Paths of Life: American Indians of the Southwest and Northern Mexico*. Tucson: University of Arizona Press, 1996.

138 Trimble, Stephen. *The People: Indians of the American Southwest*. Santa Fe: School of American Research Press, 1993.

139 Underhill, Ruth. *Papago Woman*. Prospect Heights, IL: Waveland Press, Inc., 1979.

RIVERS AND WATER CONSERVATION ISSUES

140 Bowden, Charles. *Killing the Hidden Waters*. Austin: University of Texas Press, 1977.

141 Fradkin, Philip L. *A River No More*. New York: Knopf, 1981.

142 Laney, Nancy K. *Desert Waters: From Ancient Aquifers to Modern Demands*. Tucson: Arizona-Sonora Desert Museum Press, 1998.

143 McNamee, Gregory L. *Gila: The Life and Death of an American River*. New York: Orion Books, 1994.

144 Rea, Amadeo M. *Once a River: Bird Life and Habitat Changes on the Middle Gila*. Tucson: University of Arizona Press, 1983.

145 Reisner, Marc. *Cadillac Desert: The American West and its Disappearing Water*. New York: Viking Press, 1986.

146 Tellman, Barbara. *Where to Find Water Expertise at State Universities in Arizona*. Tucson: Water Resources Research Center, University of Arizona, 1995.

147 Tellman, Barbara. *Where to Get Free (or Almost Free) Information about Water in Arizona.* Tucson: Water Resources Research Center, University of Arizona, 1994.

148 Tellman, Barbara, Richard Yarde, and Mary G. Wallace. *Arizona's Changing Rivers: How People Have Affected the Rivers.* Tucson: Water Resources Research Center, University of Arizona, 1997.

ATMOSPHERIC PHENOMENA

149 Bohren, Craig F. *Clouds in a Glass of Beer: Simple Experiments in Atmospheric Physics.* New York: John Wiley and Sons, Inc., 1987.

150 Ludlum, David M. *National Audubon Society Field Guide to North American Weather.* New York: Alfred A. Knopf, Inc., 1995.

151 Meinel, Aden and Marjorie. *Sunsets, Twilights, and Evening Skies.* Cambridge, Great Britain: Cambridge University Press, 1983.

152 Minnaert, Marcel G. J. *Light and Color in the Outdoors.* New York: Springer-Verlag, 1993.

153 Schaefer, Vincent J., and John A. Day. *A Field Guide to the Atmosphere.* Boston: Houghton Mifflin Co., 1981. (Peterson Field Guide Series)

HIKING, CAMPING, AND TRAVEL

154 Aitchison, Stewart, and Bruce Grubbs. *Hiking Arizona.* Helena, MT: Falcon Press Publishing Co., 1992.

155 Annerino, John. *Adventuring in Arizona.* San Francisco: Sierra Club Books, 1996.

156 Annerino, John. *Outdoors in Arizona: A Guide to Hiking and Backpacking.* Phoenix: Arizona Highways, 1987.

157 Beasley, Conger, Jr., Michael Collier, Frank Deckert, Dave Ganci, Robert Gildart, Daniel Murphy, Jeremy Schmidt, and Stephen Trimble. *The Sierra Club Guides to the National Parks: The Desert Southwest.* New York: Random House, Inc., 1996.

158 Bridges, Fraser. *Natural Places of the Southwest: A Traveler's Guide to the Culture, Spirit, and Ecology of Scenic Destinations.* Rocklin, CA: Prima Publishing, 1996.

159 Brown, Ann-Marie. *Southwest Camping.* San Francisco: Foghorn Press, 1994.

160 Brown, Joseph E., Barbara B. Decker, Robert E. Decker, David Lavender, Susanna Margolis, and William Truesdell. *The Sierra Club Guides to the National Parks: California, Hawaii, and American Samoa.* New York: Random House, Inc., 1996.

161 Carr, John N. *Arizona Wildlife Viewing Guide.* Helena, MT: Falcon Press, 1992.

162 Clark, Jeanne L. *California Wildlife Viewing Guide.* Helena, MT: Falcon Press, 1996.

163 Cunningham, Bill, and Polly Burke. *Hiking California's Desert Parks.* Helena, MT: Falcon Press Publishing Co., 1996.

164 Ferranti, Philip, Bruce Hagerman, and Denice Hagerman. *75 Great Hikes In and Near Palm Springs and the Coachella Valley*. Dubuque: Kendall/Hunt Publishing Company, 1995.

165 Fletcher, Colin. *The Complete Walker III*. New York: Alfred A.Knopf, 1996.

166 Foster, Lynne. *Adventuring in the California Desert*. San Francisco: Sierra Club Books, 1987.

167 Furbush, Patty A. *On Foot in Joshua Tree National Park: A Comprehensive Hiking Guide*. Lebanon, ME: M. I. Adventure Publications, 1995.

168 Ganci, Dave. *Arizona Day Hikes*. San Francisco: Sierra Club Books, 1995.

169 Hodgson, Michael. *The Basic Essentials of Minimizing Impact on the Wilderness*. Merrillville, IN: ICS Books, Inc., 1991.

170 Holing, Dwight. *The Smithsonian Guides to Natural America: The Far West—California and Nevada*. Washington, D.C.: Smithsonian Books, 1996.

171 Holt, Harold R. *A Birder's Guide to Southern California*. Colorado Springs: American Birding Association, 1990.

172 Krist, John. *50 Best Short Hikes in California Deserts*. Berkeley: Wilderness Press, 1995.

173 Leavengood, Betty. *Tucson Hiking Guide*. Boulder, CO: Pruett Publishing Co., 1997.

174 Lindsay, Lowell and Diana. *The Anza-Borrego Desert Region*. Berkeley: Wilderness Press, 1995.

175 McKinney, John. *Walking California's Desert Parks: A Day Hiker's Guide*. San Francisco: Harper Collins, 1996.

176 Molvar, Erik. *Hiking Arizona's Cactus Country*. Helena, MT: Falcon Press Publishing Co., 1995.

177 Murray, John A. *Cactus Country: An Illustrated Guide*. Boulder, CO: Roberts Rinehart Publishers, 1996.

178 Page, Jake. *The Smithsonian Guides to Natural America: The Southwest—New Mexico and Arizona*. Washington, D.C.: Smithsonian Books, 1995.

179 Perry, John, and Jane Greverus Perry. *The Sierra Club Guide to the Natural Areas of California*. San Francisco: Sierra Club Books, 1997.

180 Perry, John, and Jane Greverus Perry. *The Sierra Club Guide to the Natural Areas of New Mexico, Arizona, And Nevada*. San Francisco: Sierra Club Books, 1985.

181 Riley, Laura and William. *Guide to the National Wildlife Refuges*. New York: Collier Books, 1992.

182 Schad, Jerry. *101 Hikes in Southern California: Exploring Mountains, Seashore, and Desert*. Berkeley: Wilderness Press, 1996.

183 Stocker, Joseph. *Travel Arizona: 16 Full-Color Tours of the Grand Canyon State*. Phoenix: Arizona Highways, 1983.

184 Taylor, Richard Cachor. *A Birder's Guide to Southeastern Arizona*. Colorado Springs: American Birding Association, 1995.

185 Tucson Audubon Society Publications Committee. *Davis and Russell's Finding Birds in Southeast Arizona.* Tucson: Tucson Audubon Society, 1995.

186 Warren, Scott S. *100 Hikes in Arizona.* Seattle: The Mountaineers, 1994.

187 Warren, Scott S. *Exploring Arizona's Wild Areas: A Guide for Hikers, Backpackers, Climbers, X-C Skiers & Paddlers.* Seattle: The Mountaineers, 1996.

SPECIAL TOPICS

188 Betancourt, Julio L., Thomas R. Van Devender, and Paul S. Martin. *Packrat Middens: The Last 40,000 Years of Biotic Change.* Tucson: University of Arizona Press, 1990.

189 Buchmann, Stephen L., and Gary Paul Nabhan. *The Forgotten Pollinators.* Washington, D.C.: Island Press, 1996.

190 Cockrum, E. Lendell. *Rabies, Lyme Disease, Hanta Virus and Other Animal-Borne Human Diseases in the United States and Canada: What every Parent, Householder, Camper, Hiker, Teacher, Wildlife Rehabilitator, Hunter and Fisherman Needs to Know.* Tucson: Fisher Books: 1997.

191 Dahl, Kevin. *Wild Foods of the Sonoran Desert.* Tucson: Arizona-Sonora Desert Museum Press, 1995.

192 Guterson, Ben. *Seasonal Guide to the Year: A Month by Month Guide to Natural Events: Colorado, New Mexico, Arizona and Utah.* Golden, CO: Fulcrum Publishing, 1994.

193 Halvorson, William L., and Gary E. Davis, eds. *Science and Ecosystem Management in the National Parks.* Tucson: University of Arizona Press, 1996.

194 Hanson, Roseann Beggy, and Jonathan Hanson. *Southern Arizona Nature Almanac.* Boulder, CO: Pruett Publishing Co., 1996.

195 Hastings, James Rodney, and Raymond M. Turner. *The Changing Mile.* Tucson: University of Arizona Press, 1965.

196 Hornaday, William T. *Camp-fires on Desert and Lava.* Tucson: University of Arizona Press, 1983. (First published 1908.)

197 Lowe, Charles H. *Arizona's Natural Environment: Landscapes and Habitats.* Tucson: University of Arizona Press, 1964.

198 McGinnies, William M. *Discovering the Desert: The Legacy of the Carnegie Desert Botanical Laboratory.* Tucson: University of Arizona Press, 1981.

199 Miller, Tom, ed. *Arizona: The Land and the People.* Tucson: University of Arizona Press, 1986.

200 Webb, Robert H. *Grand Canyon, A Century of Change: Rephotography of the 1889-1890 Stanton Expedition.* Tucson: University of Arizona Press, 1996.

ORGANIZATIONS

To find out which of the organizations listed here have information related to a specific question in this book, see Appendix G: Additional Sources. The organizations are numbered for reference in that appendix.

Lists like this one inevitably lose accuracy after they're published. Internet addresses—uniform resource locators or URLs—are particularly changeable. If a URL listed here has become inactive, or if none is given for an organization, you can look for a URL by using a search engine like Alta Vista (http://www.altavista.digital.com).

Of course, search engines can also help you find much additional information on the Internet, independent of the organizations listed here.

We'd appreciate your help in bringing this list up to date for the next edition. If you notice an error or have an addition to suggest, please let us know by writing:

Publications/Book of Answers
Arizona-Sonora Desert Museum
2021 N. Kinney Rd.
Tucson, AZ 85743-8918

SPECIAL INTEREST ORGANIZATIONS

PLANTS —

1 **Arizona Native Plant Society**
Box 41206 Sun Station
Tucson, AZ 85717
http://www.azstarnet.com/~anps

2 **California Native Plant Society**
http://www.calpoly.edu/~dchippin/
cnps_main.html
CNPS Los Angeles-Santa Monica
Mountains Chapter

6233 Lubao Ave.
Woodland Hills, CA 91367
(818) 881-3706

CNPS Riverside-San Bernardino
Chapter
Inquire at San Diego Chapter (below)

CNPS San Diego Chapter
c/o San Diego Natural History Museum
P.O. Box 1390
San Diego, CA 92112-1390
(760) 665-7321
http://www.san.rr.com/cnpssd

INSECTS AND THEIR RELATIVES —

3 **Lorquin Entomological Society**
Natural History Museum of
Los Angeles: Insect Zoo
900 Exposition Blvd.
Los Angeles, CA 90007
(213) 763-3558
http://www.lam.mus.ca.us/~lorquin

4 **Sonoran Arthropod Studies Institute**
P.O. Box 5624, Tucson, AZ 85703
(520) 883-3945
http://www.azstarnet.com/~sasi

AMPHIBIANS AND REPTILES —

5 **Arizona Herpetological Association**
P.O. Box 66712
Phoenix, AZ 85082-6712
(602) 894-1625
http://www.syspac.com/~varney/
aha.html

6 **National Turtle and Tortoise Society**
P.O. Box 66935
Phoenix, AZ 85082-6935
(602) 967-6295
http://www.syspac.com/~varney/
NETSCAPE/NTTS/ntts.html

7 **San Diego Herpetological Society**
P.O. Box 4036
San Diego, CA 92164-4036
(619) 474-5553
http://www.syspac.com/~varney/
   NETSCAPE/SDHS/sdhs.html

8 **Southern California
Herpetology Association**
P.O. Box 90083
Long Beach, CA 90809-0083
http://www.syspac.com/~varney/
   NETSCAPE/SCHA/scha.html

9 **Southwestern Herpetologists Society**
P.O. Box 7469, Van Nuys, CA 91409
http://www.swhs.org

10 **Tucson Herpetological Society**
P.O. Box 709
Tucson, AZ 85702-0709
http://www.azstarnet.com/~
   bsavary/THSpage.html

BIRDS —

11 **National Audubon Society**
http://www.audubon.org

Arizona --

Arizona Audubon Council
516 E. Portland St.
Phoenix, AZ 85004
(602) 252-4339

Maricopa Audubon Society
P.O. Box 15451
Phoenix, AZ 85060

Tucson Audubon Society
300 E. University Blvd., #120
Tucson, AZ 85705
(520) 629-0510

Yuma County Audubon Society
P.O. Box 6395
Yuma, AZ 85364-6395

California —

National Audubon Society—California
555 Audubon Place
Sacramento, CA 95825
(916) 481-5332
http://www.audubon-ca.org

Palomar Audubon Society
P.O. Box 2483
Escondido, CA 92033
(619) 487-2464

San Bernardino Valley
Audubon Society
San Bernardino County Museum
2024 Orange Tree Ln.
Redlands, CA 92374

San Diego Audubon Society
2321 Morena Blvd., Suite D
San Diego, CA 92110
(619) 275-0557

RIPARIAN COMMUNITIES —

12 **Arizona Riparian Council**
Center for Environmental Studies
Box 873211
Arizona State University
Tempe, AZ 85287-3211
(602) 965-2490

HIKING AND TRAILS —

13 **Amigos de Anza**
1350 Castle Rock Rd.
Walnut Creek, CA 94598

14 **Anza Trail Coalition of Arizona**
P.O. Box 42612
Tucson, AZ 85733-2612
(520) 325-0909

15 **Arizona Trail Association**
P.O. Box 36736, Phoenix, AZ 85067
(602) 252-4794
http://www.primenet.com/~aztrail

16 Coachella Valley Hiking Club
P.O. Box 10750
Palm Desert, CA 92255

17 Coachella Valley Wanderers
52015 Ave. Martinez
La Quinta, CA 92253
(760) 564-0995

**18 Green Valley
Recreational Hiking Club**
P.O. Box 1074
Green Valley, AZ 85622

19 Pima Trails Association
P.O. Box 41358, Tucson, AZ 85717
(520) 577-7919

20 Senior Trekkers Club
250 N. Maguire Ave., Apt. 417
Tucson, AZ 85710
(520) 296-7795

21 Sierra Club
http://www.sierraclub.org

Arizona —

Grand Canyon Chapter
516 E. Portland St.
Phoenix, AZ 85004
(602) 253-8633

California —

San Diego Chapter
3820 Ray St.
San Diego, CA 92104
(619) 299-1744

San Gorgonio Chapter
568 N. Mountain View Ave./Suite 130
San Bernardino, CA 92401
(909) 381-5015

22 Southern Arizona Hiking Club
P.O. Box 32257
Tucson, AZ 85751
(520) 751-4513

23 Tucson Volkssport Klub
270 S. Chandler Dr.
Tucson, AZ 85748-6743
(520) 298-4340
http://dizzy.library.arizona.edu/users/
mount/tvk43.htm

**24 University of Arizona
Ramblers Hiking Club**
UA Student Union Activities Center
University of Arizona
Tucson, AZ 85721
(520) 621-8046

25 Valley Volkssport Association
101 N. 38th St., #30
Mesa, AZ 85205-8526
(602) 641-7577

MUSEUMS, NATURE CENTERS, AND BOTANICAL GARDENS

Arizona —

26 Arizona Historical Society Museum
949 E. 2nd St., Tucson, AZ 85719
(520) 628-5774
http://www.azstarnet.com/~azhist

27 Arizona State Museum
University of Arizona
Tucson, AZ 85721-0026
(520) 621-6281
http://w3.arizona.edu/~asm

28 Arizona-Sonora Desert Museum
2021 N. Kinney Rd.
Tucson, AZ 85743-8918
(520) 883-1380
http://www.desert.net/museum

**29 Boyce Thompson Southwestern
Arboretum**
37615 Hwy. 60, Superior, AZ 85273
(520) 689-2811
http://ag.arizona.edu/BTA

30 **Desert Botanical Garden**
1201 N. Galvin Parkway
Phoenix, AZ 85008-3490
(602) 941-1225
http://www.mobot.org/AABGA/
    Member. pages/desert.html

31 **Gila River Indian Arts and Crafts
Center and Heritage Museum**
P.O. Box 457, Sacaton, AZ 85247
(I-10 Exit 175)
(602) 963-3981 or (520) 315-3411

32 **The Heard Museum**
22 E. Monte Vista Rd.
Phoenix, AZ 85004-1480
(602) 252-8840
http://www.heard.org

33 **Mesa Southwest Museum**
53 N. MacDonald St., Mesa, AZ 85201
(602) 644-2230
http://www.ci.mesa.az.us/parksrec/msm

34 **Pueblo Grande Museum
and Cultural Park**
4619 E. Washington St.
Phoenix, AZ 85034
(602) 495-0900
http://www.arizonaguide.com/
    pueblogrande

35 **Tohono Chul Park**
7366 N. Paseo del Norte
Tucson, AZ 85704
(520) 742-6455
http://www.emol.org/emol/tucson/
    tohonochulpark
http://aabga.mobot.org/AABGA/
    Member.pages/tohono.chul.pk.html

36 **Tucson Botanical Gardens**
2150 N. Alvernon, Tucson, AZ 85712
(520) 326-9255
http://aabga.mobot.org/AABGA/
    Member.pages/tuscon.bot.gdn.html

California —

37 **Agua Caliente Cultural Museum**
219 S. Palm Canyon Dr.
Palm Springs, CA 92262
(760) 323-0151
http://www.primenet.com/accmuseum

38 **Coachella Valley Museum
and Cultural Center**
82-616 Miles Ave., Indio, CA 92201
(760) 342-6651

39 **Hi-Desert Nature Museum**
57116 Twentynine Palms Hwy.
Yucca Valley, CA 92284
(760) 369-7212

40 **Imperial Valley College
Desert Museum**
P.O. Box 430, Ocotillo, CA 92259
(760) 358-7016
http://www.imperial.cc.ca.us/ivc-dm/
    ivcdm.htm

41 **The Living Desert Wildlife and
Botanical Park**
47-900 Portola Ave.
Palm Desert, CA 92260
(760) 346-5694
http://palmsprings.com/points/
    desert.html

42 **Moorten Botanical Gardens**
1701 S. Palm Canyon Dr.
Palm Springs, CA 92264
(760) 327-6555

43 **Needles Regional Museum**
923 Front St., Needles, CA 92363
(760) 326-5678

44 **Palm Springs Desert Museum**
101 Museum Dr.
Palm Springs, CA 92262
(760) 325-0189
http://www.psmuseum.org

45 San Bernardino County Museum
2024 Orange Tree Ln.
Redlands, CA 92374
1-888-BIRD EGG
(909) 798-8570
http://www.co.sanbernardino.ca.us/
ccr/museum/museums.htm

46 San Diego Natural History Museum
P.O. Box 1390, San Diego, CA 92112
(619) 232-3821
http://www.sdnhm.org

PRIVATE LAND PRESERVATION ORGANIZATIONS

47 The Nature Conservancy
http://www.tnc.org

Arizona offices —

Arizona Field Office
300 E. University Blvd., Suite 230
Tucson, AZ 85705
(520) 622-3861

Phoenix Office
5308 N. 12th St., Suite 402
Phoenix, AZ 85011
(602) 264-4665

Arizona preserves —

Aravaipa Canyon Preserve
Klondyke Station, Willcox, AZ 85643
(520) 828-3443

Hassayampa River Preserve
Box 1162
Wickenburg, AZ 85358
(520) 684-2772

Muleshoe Ranch
Cooperative Management Area
R.R. #1, Box 1542
Willcox, AZ 85643
(520) 586-7072

Patagonia-Sonoita Creek Preserve
P.O. Box 815, Patagonia, AZ 85624
(520) 394-2400

Ramsey Canyon Preserve
27 Ramsey Canyon Rd.
Hereford, AZ 85615
(520) 378-2785

California offices —

California Regional Office
201 Mission St., 4th Floor
San Francisco, CA 94105
(415) 777-0487

Southern California Office
27393 Ynez Rd., #251
Temequila, CA 92591
(909) 699-1856

California preserves —

Big Morongo Canyon Preserve
Box 780
Morongo Valley, CA 92256
(760) 363-7190

Coachella Valley Preserve
P.O. Box 188
Thousand Palms, CA 92276
(760) 343-1234

Dos Palmas Oasis Preserve
(contact Coachella Valley Preserve)

FEDERAL AGENCIES

48 Bureau of Land Management, USDI
http://www.blm.gov

Arizona offices and points of interest —
http://azwww.az.blm.gov

Arizona State Office
222 N. Central Ave.
Phoenix, AZ 85004
(602) 650-0500

Kingman Field Office
2475 Beverly Ave.
Kingman, AZ 86401
(520) 757-3161
  • Burro Creek Recreation Area

Lake Havasu Field Office
2610 Sweetwater Ave
Lake Havasu City, AZ 86406
(520) 505-1200
  • Parker Dam Road
    Back Country Byway
  • Swansea Ghost Town

Phoenix Field Office
2015 W. Deer Valley Rd.
Phoenix, AZ 85027-2099
(602) 580-5500
  • Black Canyon Trail
  • Harquahala Peak Observatory
  • Painted Rocks Recreation Area

Safford Field Office
711 14th Ave., Safford, AZ 85546
(520) 348-4400
  • Aravaipa Canyon Wilderness
  • Black Hills Back Country Byway
  • Gila Box Riparian National
    Conservation Area
  • Hot Well Dunes

Tucson Field Office
12611 E. Broadway Blvd.
Tucson, AZ 85748
(520) 722-4289
  • Empire-Cienega Resource
    Conservation Area
  • San Pedro Riparian National
    Conservation Area

Yuma Field Office
2555 E. Gila Ridge Rd.
Yuma, AZ 85365
(520) 317-3200
  • Betty's Kitchen Interpretive Trail
  • Blythe Intaglios (in California)

  • Imperial Dam Long-Term Visitor
    Area (in California)
  • La Posa Long-Term Visitor Area

California offices and points of interest —
http://www.ca.blm.gov/caso

California State Office
2135 Butano Way
Sacramento, CA 95825
(916) 978-4400

El Centro Resource Area
1661 4th St.
El Centro, CA 92243
(760) 337-4400
  • Dunes Vista
    Long-Term Visitor Area
  • Hot Spring
    Long-Term Visitor Area
  • North Algodones Dunes
    Wilderness Area
  • Pilot Knob
    Long-Term Visitor Area
  • Tamarisk
    Long-Term Visitor Area

Needles Resource Area
101 W. Spikes Rd.
Needles, CA 92363
(760) 326-7600

Palm Springs-South Coast
  Resource Area
P.O. Box 2000
(690 W. Garnet Ave.)
Palm Springs, CA 92258
(760) 251-4800
  • Big Morongo Canyon Preserve
    (see also The Nature Conservancy:
    Big Morongo Canyon Preserve)
  • Coachella Valley Fringe-toed
  • Lizard Preserve
    (see also The Nature Conservancy:
    Coachella Valley Preserve)
  • Midland Long-Term Visitor Area

• Mule Mountain
Long-Term Visitor Area
• Santa Rosa Mountains
National Scenic Area

49 National Park Service, USDI
http://www.nps.gov

Casa Grande Ruins
National Monument
1100 Ruins Drive
Coolidge, AZ 85228
(520) 723-3172

Hohokam Pima National Monument
c/o Casa Grande Ruins National
Monument

Joshua Tree National Park
74485 National Park Dr.
Twentynine Palms, CA 92277
(760) 367-5500

Organ Pipe Cactus
National Monument
Rt. 1, Box 100
Ajo, AZ 85321-9626
(520) 387-6849

Saguaro National Park
3693 S. Old Spanish Trail
Tucson, AZ 85730-5601
520-733-5153

Tonto National Monument
HC02 Box 4602
Roosevelt, AZ 85545
(520) 467-2241

50 U.S. Fish and Wildlife Service, USDI
1849 C. St., NW, MIB 3012
Washington, D.C. 20240
(202) 208-4717
http://www.fws.gov

Regional offices —

Region 1 (includes California)
911 NE 11th Ave.
Eastside Federal Complex
Portland, OR 97232-4181
(503) 231-6618

Region 2 (includes Arizona)
P.O. Box 1306
Albuquerque, NM 87103
(505) 248-6282

National Wildlife Refuges —
http://refuges.fws.gov

Bill Williams NWR
60911 Highway 95
Parker, AZ 85344
(520) 667-4144

Buenos Aires NWR
P.O. Box 109, Sasabe, AZ 85633
(520) 823-4251

Cabeza Prieta NWR
1611 N. Second Ave., Ajo, AZ 85321
(520) 387-6483

Cibola NWR
P.O. Box AP
Blythe, CA 92226
(520) 857-3253

Coachella Valley NWR
Contact Salton Sea NWR or
The Nature Conservancy:
Coachella Valley Preserve

Havasu NWR
P.O. Box 3009
Needles, CA 92363
(760) 326-3853

Imperial NWR
P.O. Box 72217
Yuma, AZ 85365
(520) 783-3371

Kofa NWR
P.O. Box 6290, Yuma, AZ 85366-6290
(520) 783-7861

Salton Sea NWR
906 W. Sinclair Rd.
Calipatria, CA 92233-0120
(760) 348-5278

U.S. DEPARTMENT OF AGRICULTURE

51 Forest Service, USDA
http://www.fs.fed.us

Cleveland National Forest
10845 Rancho Bernardo Rd.
San Diego, CA 92127-2107
(619) 673-6180

Coronado National Forest
300 W. Congress, Tucson, AZ 85701
(520) 670-4552

Prescott National Forest
344 S. Cortez St.
Prescott, AZ 86303-4398
(520) 771-4700

San Bernardino National Forest
1824 S. Commercenter Circle
San Bernardino, CA 92408
(909) 383-5588

Tonto National Forest
2324 E. McDowell Rd.
Phoenix, AZ 85006
(602) 225-5200

STATE WILDLIFE MANAGEMENT AGENCIES

52 Arizona Game and Fish Department
2221 W. Greenway Rd.
Phoenix, AZ 85023-4339
(602) 942-3000
http://www.gf.state.az.us

Regional offices and wildlife areas —

Region III
5235 N. Stockton Hill Rd.
Kingman, AZ 86401
(520) 692-7700

Region IV
9140 E. County 10-1/2 St.
Yuma, AZ 85365
(520) 342-0091
  • Alamo Wildlife Area
    (see Alamo Lake State Park)
  • Mittry Lake Wildlife Area

Region V
555 N. Greasewood Rd.
Tucson, AZ 85745
(520) 628-5376
  • Cluff Ranch Wildlife Area
    (520) 485-9430

Region VI
7200 E. University Dr.
Mesa, AZ 85207
602-981-9400
  • Arlington Wildlife Area
  • Base Meridian Amator
    Wildlife Area
  • Robins Butte Wildlife Area
  • Roosevelt Lake Wildlife Area

53 California
Department of Fish and Game
1416 9th St.
Sacramento, CA 95814
(916) 653-7664
http://www.dfg.ca.gov

Region Five
(includes southern California)
330 Golden Shore, Suite 50
Long Beach, CA 90802
(562) 590-5132
  • Imperial Wildlife Area
    (760) 359-0577

STATE PARKS

54 Arizona State Parks
1300 W. Washington
Phoenix, AZ 85007
(602) 542-4174
http://www.pr.state.az.us

Alamo Lake State Park
Box 38
Wenden, AZ 85357
(520) 669-2088

Boyce Thompson Southwestern
   Arboretum
(see under Museums, Nature Centers
and Botanical gardens)

Buckskin Mountain State Park
54761 Highway 95
Parker, AZ 85344
(520) 667-3231

Catalina State Park
Box 36986
Tucson, AZ 85740
(520) 628-5798

Cattail Cove State Park
P.O. Box 1990
Lake Havasu City, AZ 86405
(520) 855-1223

Kartchner Caverns State Park
Contact state parks office:
(602) 542-4174

Lake Havasu State Park
1801 Hwy. 95
Lake Havasu City, AZ 86406
Administration building:
(520) 855-7851
Windsor Beach Ranger Station:
(520) 855-2784

Lost Dutchman State Park
6109 N. Apache Trail

Apache Junction, AZ 85219
(602) 982-4485

McFarland Historical State Park
Box 109
Florence, AZ 85232
(520) 868-5216

Oracle
Center for Environmental Education
P.O. Box 700
Oracle, AZ 85623
(520) 896-2425

Picacho Peak State Park
Box 275
Picacho Peak, AZ 85241
(520) 466-3183

Roper Lake State Park
Rt. 2, Box 712
Safford, AZ
(520) 428-6760

Yuma Crossing State Historic Park
201 N. 4th Ave.
Yuma, AZ 85364
(520) 329-0471

Yuma Territorial Prison
State Historic Park
Box 10792
Yuma, AZ 85366-8792
(520) 783-4771

55 California
State Parks and Recreation Areas
The Resources Agency
1416 9th St.
Sacramento, CA 95814
(916) 653-6995
http://ceres.ca.gov/parks/dpr.html

Anza-Borrego Desert State Park
200 Palm Springs Drive
Borrego Springs, CA 92004
(760) 767-5311

Indio Hills Palms
Contact The Nature Conservancy:
Coachella Valley Preserve

Mount San Jacinto State Park
P.O. Box 308 (25905 Highway 243)
Idyllwild, CA 92549
(909) 659-2607

Picacho State Recreation Area
P.O. Box 848, Winterhaven, CA 92283
(760) 393-3059

Salton Sea State Recreation Area
100-225 State Park Rd.
North Shore, CA 92254
(760) 393-1338

COUNTY PARKS

Arizona —

56 La Paz County Parks
7350 Riverside Dr.
Parker, AZ 85344
(520) 667-2069
  • Bouse Park
  • Centennial Park
  • La Paz County Park
  • Patria Flats Day Use Park

57 Maricopa County
Parks and Recreation
3475 W. Durango St.
Phoenix, AZ 85009
(602) 506-2930
http://www.maricopa.gov
  • Cave Creek Recreation Area
  • Estrella Mountain Regional Park
  • Lake Pleasant Regional Park
  • McDowell Mountain
      Regional Park
  • Usery Mountain Recreation Area
  • White Tank Mountain
      Regional Park
  • San Tan Mountains Regional Park

58 Mohave
County Parks
P.O. Box 7000
Kingman, AZ 86402
(520) 757-0915
  • SARA Park

59 Pima County
Parks and Recreation Department
1024 W. Silverlake Rd.
Tucson, AZ 85713-2799
(520) 740-2690
http://www.azstar.com/~pcpr
  • Colossal Cave Mountain Park
  • Cienega Creek Natural Preserve
  • Roy Drachman/Agua Caliente
      Regional Park
  • Tortolita Mountain Park
  • Tucson Mountain Park

60 Pinal County
Parks and Recreation
P.O. Box 3110 11 MCRB
(512 S. 11 Mile Corner Rd.)
Casa Grande, AZ 85222
(520) 723-5242
  • Oracle Park
  • West Pinal Park (Kortson Park)

California —

61 Imperial County
Parks and Recreation
County Property Services
1002 State St.
El Centro, CA 92243
(760) 339-4384
  • Red Hill Marina County Park

62 Riverside County
Regional Parkand Open Space District
P.O. Box 3507
Riverside, CA 92159-3507
http://www.co.riverside.ca.us/
    activity/parks
  • Blythe Marina Recreation Area

- Fish Traps Archeological Site
- Goose Flats Wildlife Area
- Lake Cahuilla Recreation Area
- Mayflower Park
- McIntyre Park

63 San Bernardino County
Community and Cultural Resources
Regional Parks
777 E. Rialto Ave.
San Bernardino, Ca 92415-0673
(909) 387-2757
- Moabi Regional Park
- Morongo Wildlife Reserve
  (see also The Nature Conservancy:
  Big Morongo Canyon Preserve)

64 San Diego County
Parks and Recreation
County Operations Center Annex
5201 Ruffin Rd., Suite P
San Diego, CA 92123
(619) 694-3030
- Agua Caliente County Park
- Vallecito Regional Park

STATE AGRICULTURE DEPARTMENTS

For information about legal protection
of native plants.

65 Arizona Department of Agriculture
Native Plant Division
1688 W. Adams
Phoenix, AZ 85007
1-800-645-5440
http://agriculture.state.az.us

66 California
Department of Food and Agriculture
http://www.cdfa.ca.gov

County Agricultural Commissioners —

Imperial County
Agricultural Commissioner

150 S. 9th St.
El Centro, CA 92243-2801
(760) 339-4314

Riverside County
Agricultural Commissioner
P.O. Box 1089
(4080 Lemon St., Room 19)
Riverside, CA 92502-1089
(909) 275-3045

San Bernardino County
Agricultural Commissioner
777 E. Rialto Ave.
San Bernardino, CA 92415-0720
(909) 387-2105

San Diego County
Agricultural Commissioner
5555 Overland Ave., Building 3
San Diego, CA 92123-1292
(619) 694-2739

COOPERATIVE EXTENSION PROGRAMS

67 Arizona Cooperative Extension
University of Arizona
Forbes Building, Room 301
Tucson, AZ 85721
(520) 621-7205
http://ag.arizona.edu/Ext

Gila County Extension
1177 Monroe St.
Globe, AZ 85501-1415
(520) 425-7179

Graham County Extension
P.O. Box 127
Solomon, AZ 85551-0127
(520) 428-2611

La Paz County Extension
P.O. Box BL, Parker, AZ 85344-4064
(520) 669-9843

Maricopa County Extension
4341 E. Broadway
Phoenix, AZ 85040-8807
(602) 470-8086

Pima County Extension
4210 N. Campbell Ave.
Tucson, AZ 85719-1109
(520) 626-5161

Pinal County Extension
820 E. Cottonwood Ln., Bldg. C
Casa Grande, AZ 85222-2276
(520) 836-5221

Yavapai County Extension
P.O. Box 388
Prescott, AZ 86302-0388
(520) 445-6590

Yuma County Extension
198 S. Main St., 3rd Floor
Yuma, AZ 85364-1424
(520) 329-2150

68 University of California
Cooperative Extension
Division of Agriculture and
    Natural Resources
Southern Region
Riverside, CA 92521
http://uccesouth.ucr.edu

UCCE Imperial County
1050 E. Holton Rd.
Holtville, CA 92250-9615
(760) 352-9474

UCCE Riverside County
21150 Box Springs Rd.
Moreno Valley, CA 92557-8708
(909) 683-6491

UCCE San Bernardino County
777 E. Rialto Ave.
San Bernardino, CA 92415-0730
(909) 387-2171

UCCE San Diego County
5555 Overland Ave., Bldg 4
San Diego, CA 92123-1219
(619) 694-2845

WATER CONSERVATION
INFORMATION

See also: Museums, Nature Centers, and
Botanical Gardens; Cooperative Extension
Programs; your local water utility.

Arizona —

69 Arizona Department of
Water Resources
15 S. 15th Ave., Phoenix, AZ 85007
(602) 542-1553
http://www.adwr.state.az.us

70 Arizona Municipal Water
Users Association
4041 N. Central Ave. #900
Phoenix, AZ 85012
(602) 248-8482
http://www.tempe.gov/amwua

71 Mesa Community College
Biological Sciences
    Demonstration Garden
1833 W. Southern, Mesa, AZ 85202
(602) 461-7107

72 Office of Arid Lands Studies
University of Arizona
845 N. Park Ave.
Tucson, AZ 85719
(520) 621-1955
http://www.ag.arizona.edu/
    OALS/oals

73 City of Phoenix
Water Services Departments
200 W. Washington 9th Floor
Phoenix, AZ 85003-1611
(602) 262-6627

74 **Salt River Project**
P.O. Box 52025
Phoenix, AZ 85072
(602) 236-3333

75 **Southern Arizona**
Water Resources Association
48 N. Tucson Blvd., #106
Tucson, AZ 85716
(520) 881-3939
http://www.scottnet.com/sawara

76 **Tucson Water**
P.O. Box 27210, Tucson, AZ 85726
(520) 791-4331
http://www.ci.tucson.az/water

77 **Water Resources Research Center**
College of Agriculture
University of Arizona
350 N. Campbell Ave.
Tucson, AZ 85721
(520) 792-9591
http://ag.arizona.edu/azwater

California —

78 **American Water Works Association**
California-Nevada Section
1225 S. Bon View Ave.
Ontario, CA 91761
http://www.awwa.org

79 **California**
Department of Water Resources
Office of Water Education
P.O. Box 942836, Room 1104-2
Sacramento, CA 94236-0001
(916) 653-6192
http://wwwdwr.water.ca.gov

80 **Desert Water Agency**
P.O. Box 1710
Palm Springs, CA 92263
(760) 323-4971
http://www.dwa.org

81 **Water Education Foundation**
717 K St., Suite 517
Sacramento, CA 95814
(916) 444-6240
http://www.water-ed.org

POISON CONTROL SYSTEMS

82 **Arizona Poison Control System**
1-800-362-0101

83 **California Poison Control System**
1-800-876-4766

STATE HEALTH DEPARTMENTS

84 **Arizona**
Department of Health Services
Disease Prevention
3815 N. Black Canyon Hwy.
Phoenix, AZ 85015
602-230-5817

85 **California**
Department of Health Services
P.O. Box 942732
(714/744 P St.)
Sacramento, CA 94234-7320
(916) 323-2333
http://www.dhs.cahwnet.gov

COUNTY HEALTH DEPARTMENTS

Arizona —

86 **Gila County Health Department**
1400 E. Ash St. (mailing address)
621 S. 5th St. (physical location)
Globe, AZ 85501
520-425-3189

87 **Graham County Health Department**
826 W. Main, Safford, AZ 85546
520-428-0110

88 La Paz County Health Department
916 12th St., Parker, AZ 85344
520-669-6155

89 Maricopa County
Department of Public Health
1825 E. Roosevelt, Phoenix, AZ 85006
602-506-6868

90 Mohave County Health Department
305 W. Beale, Kingman, AZ 86401
520-753-0748

91 Pima County
Public Health Department
150 W. Congress, Tucson, AZ 85701
520-740-8315

92 Pinal County Health Department
188 S. Main, Coolidge, AZ 85228
520-723-9541

93 Yavapai County Health Department
930 Division St.
Prescott, AZ 85301
520-771-3122

94 Yuma County Health Department
201 2nd Ave., Yuma, AZ 85364
520-329-2220

California —

95 Imperial County
Health Department
935 Broadway
El Centro, CA 92243-2396
(760) 339-4438

96 Riverside County
Public Health Department
Health and Administration Building
4065 County Circle Dr.
Riverside, CA 92503
(909) 358-5058
http://www.co.riverside.ca.us/
depts/health

97 San Bernardino County
Health Department
351 N. Mountain View Ave.
San Bernardino, CA 92415-0010
(909) 387-6280
http://www.co.san-bernardino.ca.us/
sbco/health.htm

98 San Diego County
Health Services Department
1700 Pacific Coast Highway
San Diego, CA 92101
(619) 515-6770
http://www.co.san-diego.ca.us/cnty/
cntydepts/health/services

OTHER HEALTH-RELATED ORGANIZATIONS

99 American Red Cross
http://www.redcross.org

Arizona —
(800) 842-7349
(ask for Health and Safety)

Central Arizona Chapter
6135 N. Black Canyon Highway
Phoenix, AZ 85015
(602) 336-6660
http://aztec.asu.edu/arc

Southern Arizona Chapter
3915 E. Broadway Blvd., #300
Tucson, AZ 85711
(520) 318-6740
http://www.azsunset.com/sarc

California —

High Desert Chapter
16248 Desert Knoll Dr.
Victorville, CA 92392-0412
760-245-6511
http://www.brigadoon.com/~archdc

Inland Empire East Chapter
202 W. Rialto Ave.
San Bernardino, CA 92408
(909) 888-1481

Morongo Basin Chapter
6416 Hallee Rd.
P.O. Box 212
Joshua Tree, CA 92252
760-366-5330

Riverside Chapter
74140 El Paseo, Suite 2
Palm Desert, CA 92260
760-773-9105

San Diego/Imperial Counties
    Chapter
3650 5th Ave.
San Diego, CA 92103-4220
(619) 542-7400

100 **Centers for Disease Control
and Prevention**
1600 Clifton Rd., NE
Atlanta, GA 30333
(404) 639-3311
http://www.cdc.gov

101 **Valley Fever Center for Excellence**
Veterans Affairs Medical Center (111)
3601 S. 6th Ave.
Tucson, AZ 85723
(520) 629-4777
(800) 470-8262 (from Arizona only)
http://www.arl.arizona.edu/vfce

GLOSSARY

Adaptation: The process in *evolution* by which living things become fitted to their environment by genetic changes in their anatomy, physiology, or behavior. For example, kangaroo rats have adapted to deserts by developing efficient kidneys that reduce urinary water loss.

Aerosol: (AIR-uh-sol) Microscopic solid particles or liquid droplets floating (suspended) in a gas. Smoke and fog are aerosols, but not all atmospheric aerosols are so easily visible.

Aestivate—see *estivate*

Alkaline soil: (AL-kuh-lun) A soil with **pH** greater than 7. Desert soils are generally alkaline because they contain salts, particularly lime (calcium carbonate, $CaCO_3$), that are leached out of soils in wetter climates. Some alkaline soils (those containing more soluble salts, such as calcium sulfate or sodium chloride) are harmful to agriculture, but many desert plants have adapted to them.

Alluvial fan: A fan-shaped deposit of *sediments* (alluvium) at the mouth of a canyon, usually deposited as slurries of mud and rock washed down during heavy rainstorms.

Altricial: (al-TRISH-ul) Helpless, nearly naked, and totally dependent on parent(s) during infancy. For example, newly hatched sparrows and newborn mice are altricial. Compare *precocial*.

Amphibian: A member of the group (class) of *vertebrates* that includes frogs, toads, and salamanders. Amphibians have moist skins without scales, and typically lay eggs in water, have aquatic larvae with gills, and terrestrial adults with lungs. Compare *reptile*.

Ak chin: (ahk cheen) A Tohono O'odham (Indian) phrase meaning "arroyo mouth," referring to a traditional method of farming that depends entirely on water that flows down arroyos into desert valleys during occasional summer rainstorms.

Anaphylaxis: (an-uh-fuh-LAK-sis) A life-threatening whole-body (systemic) allergic reaction, occurring in some persons when exposed to substances to which they've become sensitized, such as insect venoms and certain foods. Also called "anaphylactic shock."

Annual plant: A plant that completes its life cycle in a single growing season. Compare *biennial plant, perennial plant*.

Aposematic markings: (ap-uh-suh-MAT-ik) Body colors and/or patterns that signal that a living thing is dangerous. For example, the bright orange (or red or yellow) and black colors of many poisonous insects are aposematic. Also called "warning coloration."

Aquifer: An underground zone of moisture-saturated *sediments* from which water can be extracted by pumping. See also *water table*.

Arachnid: (uh-RAK-nid) A member of the group (class) of *arthropods* that includes mites, spiders, and scorpions. Arachnids have two body regions (fused head and thorax, and abdomen) and eight walking legs. Compare *insect*.

Areole: (AR-ee-ole) On a cactus, a well-defined small area on a stem, flower, or fruit where spines, leaves, flowers, and new branches arise.

Arizona Upland: The subdivision of the Sonoran Desert at its northeastern corner, characterized by moderate elevations, cooler temperatures, both summer and winter rainfall, and relatively diverse and abundant vegetation.

Arroyo: A water-carved gully or small canyon in an arid region, with vertical walls and a usually dry streambed. Compare *wash*.

Arthropod: (AR-thruh-pod) A member of a large and diverse group (phylum) of animals with *exoskeletons*, jointed legs, and segmented bodies. *Crustaceans*, millipedes, centipedes, *arachnids*, and *insects* are all arthropods.

Bajada: (buh-HA-duh) A skirt of sediments surrounding a desert mountain range, sloping gently away from the mountain front.

Belly flower: Informal term for a wild-flower so small one needs to lie on the ground to observe it.

Biennial plant: (by-EN-ee-ul) A plant that requires two growing seasons to complete its life cycle, usually flowering in the second season. Compare *annual plant, perennial plant*.

Biodiversity: Diversity in living things. Biodiversity exists on many levels, from genetic variability within a *species* to number of species in a *biotic community* and number of kinds of communities in a region. (However, the term is often used for species number alone.)

Biogeography: The study of the geographic distributions of living things.

Biome: (BY-ome) A large-scale *ecosystem* characteristic of a certain kind of climate, for example, desert (arid), tropical forest (warm and wet).

Biosphere: The largest definable *ecosystem* on earth, that is, the entire interacting system of the earth's living things and their non-living environment.

Biotic community: (by-OT-ik) The collection of interdependent living things in a given area. Biotic communities are often named for their most conspicuous plants, and called simply "communities." Example: paloverde-saguaro community.

Butte: An isolated hill with a flat top, steep sides, and a height greater than its width. Compare *mesa*.

Cactus: A member of a group (family) of plants (the Cactaceae) that typically have *succulent* stems, spines borne on *areoles*, no leaves or only *vestigial* leaves, and certain distinctive flower characteristics (e.g., many sepals and petals grading into one another, many stamens, and an inferior ovary with a multilobed stigma).

Caliche: (kuh-LEE-chee) A lime-rich soil layer, characteristic of arid regions. The lime (calcium carbonate) can take the form of powders, veins, nodules, or massive, hard deposits cementing together sediments.

CAM—see *crassulacean acid metabolism*

Canine teeth: The two pointed teeth on either side of the *incisors*. (The upper canines of a person are sometimes called "eye teeth.")

Carnivore: Any living thing that eats animal flesh. (Most carnivores are animals, but there are also carnivorous plants.) Compare *herbivore* and *omnivore*. The term can also be used for any member of the group (order Carnivora) of clawed *mammals* that includes dogs, bears, weasels, raccoons, cats, and their relatives.

Carrying capacity: The largest number of living things of a particular kind that can live in an area indefinitely without damaging it.

Chlorophyll: (KLOR-uh-fil) The green pigment in most plants as well as certain microorganisms, that captures solar energy in the process of *photosynthesis*.

Chubasco: (choo-BOS-ko) A large and severe late summer or early fall storm, often originating as a Pacific hurricane or tropical storm, that brings rain to the Sonoran Desert. (Not all thunderstorms are chubascos.)

Clone: A group of genetically identical living things, or an individual living thing that is a genetic copy of another. Many

microorganisms, plants, and lower animals reproduce asexually by cloning.

Cocci-dioidomycosis: (kok-sid-ee-oy-doh-my-KO-sis) A disease in humans and some other mammals caused by a soil fungus (*Coccidioides immitis*) prevalent in arid regions of the New World. Also called "valley fever" and "desert fever."

Coevolution: (ko-ev-uh-LOO-shun) The simultaneous *evolution* of two (or more) closely interacting *species*, such that each strongly influences the other's *adaptations*. For example, slender-billed hummingbirds have coevolved with tubular flowers, facilitating pollination.

Commensalism: A close relationship between two living things (a form of *symbiosis*) in which one benefits and the other is little affected. For example, certain desert lizards are often commensals in packrat houses; the lizards get a place to live without much affecting the packrats. Compare *mutualism, parasitism*.

Community—see *biotic community*

Convergent evolution: The evolution of similar *adaptations* in unrelated species in response to similar environmental conditions. For example, remarkably cactuslike plants with spines and succulent stems have evolved in the spurge family (Euphorbiaceae) in Old World deserts.

Crassulacean acid metabolism: (kras-you-LAY-shun) A process in which a plant opens its pores at night to take in carbon dioxide, chemically stores the gas in its tissues (as organic acids), then employs it in *photosynthesis* the following day, when its pores are closed. CAM is common in *succulents*, and it reduces water loss by *transpiration* compared to other plants, which must open their pores while performing photosynthesis during the warmer daytime hours.

Crepuscular: (kri-PUS-kew-lur) Active at twilight or dusk. Compare *diurnal, nocturnal.*

Cristate (crested) plant: A plant with an abnormal, crested form, such as the fan shape sometimes seen at the tops of saguaros.

Crop milk: A milk-like liquid produced in an organ (the crop) in the throat of pigeons and doves, and regurgitated to feed their young. Also called "pigeon's milk."

Crustacean: (kruh-STAY-shun) A member of the group (class) of *arthropods* that includes lobsters, crabs, and shrimp. Crustaceans are mostly aquatic and have hardened *exoskeletons* and two pairs of antennae.

Cryptic markings: (KRIP-tik) Camouflaging patterns or colors.

Cryptobiotic soil: (krip-toe-by-OT-ik) A dark soil crust created by a community of microorganisms, including (among others) *cyanobacteria,* algae, fungi, *lichens,* and mosses. Such living crusts add stability and nutrients to the soils on which they occur.

Cryptogamic crust: (krip-tuh-GAM-ik) see *cryptobiotic soil*

Cuticle: Term used for the outer skin or protective coating of some animals and plants.

Cyanobacteria: (SY-uh-no-bak-tir-ee-uh or sy-AN-uh-bak-tir-ee-uh) A group of bacteria bearing chlorophyll and capable of photosynthesis. An older name for cyanobacteria is "blue-green algae."

Deciduous plant: (di-SIJ-oo-us) A plant that's leafless during part of the year (i.e., isn't evergreen). See also *drought deciduous plant.*

Dendrochronologist: (den-dro-kruh-NOL-uh-jist) A scientist who uses growth rings in wood to derive dates and other information about conditions in the past, including, for example, past climates, geological events, and human prehistory. The science is called "dendrochronology."

Desert: An *ecosystem* where lack of water is severely limiting to living things most of the time. (A desert is a dry place, but not necessarily a hot one.)

Desert pavement: A soil surface layer composed of stones set closely together in a natural mosaic. Desert pavements are found on old, stable surfaces of *bajadas* and *alluvial fans,* where repeated wetting and drying of the soil has heaved rocks to the surface and wind has removed fine particles.

Desert varnish: A dark mineral glaze that coats rocks in some desert areas. Desert varnish forms over thousands of years as bacteria act on airborne dust that settles on exposed rock surfaces.

Diurnal: (dy-UR-nul) Active during the day. Compare *crepuscular* and *nocturnal.*

Drought deciduous plant: A plant that drops its leaves during dry periods.

Dust devil: A dusty whirlwind resembling a small tornado. Dust devils form when air rises over sun-heated ground and the surrounding air spirals inward to take its place, like water flowing down a drain.

Ecology: The science concerned with the relationships of living things to each other and with their non-living environment. The study of *ecosystems.*

Ecosystem: The interacting system consisting of an area's living things (*biotic community*) and the non-living (abiotic) components of their environment, such as air, water, and soil particles.

Endemic organism: (en-DEM-ik) A living thing that occurs only in a certain restricted area or region. For example, the saguaro is endemic to the Sonoran Desert.

Ephemeral plant: (i-FEM-ur-ul) A plant that completes its life cycle in a very brief period, that is, a very short-lived *annual plant.* For example, some desert ephemeral wildflowers complete their life cycles in a few weeks.

Ephemeral stream: A stream that flows only for brief periods. As an extreme example, a desert *wash* may flow for less than an hour following a rainstorm.

Epizootic: (ep-uh-zo-OT-ik) A disease outbreak in animals (the animal equivalent of an epidemic).

Erosion: The wearing away and removal of rock and soil by natural agencies like running water, ice, and wind.

Estivate: To pass a hot or very dry season in an inactive state. Estivation is the warm season counterpart of *hibernation.*

Evapotranspiration: The loss of water from the land through evaporation from soil and water surfaces as well as *transpiration* from plants.

Evolution: Technically, change in the genetic makeup of *populations* of living things over time. Such changes are usually the result of *natural selection,* resulting in *adaptation* of living things to their environment.

Exoskeleton: An external skeleton, as in insects and other *arthropods.* (An internal skeleton like ours is an "endoskeleton.")

Exotic organism: A living thing that has been introduced into an area to which it isn't native. Exotic is the opposite of *indigenous.*

Extinction: The complete disappearance of a species. An extinct species no longer exists anywhere. Compare *extirpation.*

Extirpation: The eradication of a species from a given area. Compare *extinction.*

Feral animal: (FER-ul) An domestic variety of an animal living in a wild state, for example, an escaped, free-living cat. (By analogy, a plant escaped from cultivation is sometimes called a "feral plant.")

Flash flood: A local flood or a heavy flow in a stream channel, arising suddenly, and often lasting a brief period of time. A flash flood can occur in a normally dry *wash* or *arroyo* when heavy rains fall in upstream areas, sometimes miles away from the site of flooding.

Foresummer: In the Arizona Upland subdivision of the Sonoran Desert, the hot and dry season immediately preceding the rainy summer *monsoon*.

Glochid: (GLO-kid) A small, hairlike, barbed spine found only on prickly pear and cholla cacti.

Habitat: The place, or kind of place, in which a particular kind of living thing occurs. For example, typical habitat for the creosote bush is desert plains and valley bottoms with sandy or gravelly soils.

Hantavirus: A member of a world-wide group of rodent viruses, some of which can also infect people.

Herbivore: A plant-eating animal. Compare *carnivore* and *omnivore*.

Hibernate: To pass a cold season in a state of inactivity. Compare *estivate*.

Home range: The area within which an animal travels to meet its survival needs. Compare *territory*.

Horse latitudes: A range of latitude near 30° north and south, in which descending warm, dry air tends to create a zone of high atmospheric pressure. (The term is said to have arisen among seamen during colonial times, who were forced to throw horses overboard when ships were becalmed at these latitudes and water supplies ran low.)

Incisors: The flat front teeth in mammals, necessary for cutting and pulling away food material.

Indigenous: (in-DIJ-uh-nus) Native to a particular region. For example, cacti are indigenous to the Sonoran Desert, but eucalyptus trees (originally from Australia) are not. Compare *exotic*.

Infrared: (in-fruh-RED) An invisible form of radiation beyond the red end of the visible spectrum. Infrared radiation is given off by warm objects, and can sometimes be sensed by the skin, for example if a hand is held next to a glowing coal.

Insect: A member of the large group (class) of *arthropods* that includes beetles, butterflies, and bees. Insects have a single pair of antennae, three distinct body regions (head, thorax, and abdomen), and six legs. Compare *arachnid*.

Insectivore: A living thing, usually an animal, that feeds on insects.

Invertebrate: An animal that lacks a backbone, for example a jellyfish, earthworm, or snail. Compare *vertebrate*.

IR—see *infrared*

Jacobson's organs: A pair of smell or taste organs present in many *amphibians*, *reptiles*, and *mammals*, but especially well developed in lizards and snakes, where they appear as pockets in the roof of the mouth. Some lizards and many snakes "taste the air" (and various surfaces) by flicking out their tongues, picking up odor molecules, and bringing them into the mouth to be detected by these organs.

Legume: A plant in the pea family, or the kind of fruit (a "bean pod") borne by most members of this family.

Lichen: (LY-kun) A plantlike growth, for example on tree bark or rock, consisting of an alga and a fungus living together in a close relationship (thought by most ecologists to be *mutualism*).

Life-zone: A zone of elevation and/or latitude supporting generally similar plant and animal life. For example, the Lower Sonoran Life-zone includes all areas of desert vegetation in the warm Southwestern deserts: the Mohave, the Sonoran, and the Chihuahuan. (The Upper Sonoran Life-zone includes non-desert communities like grasslands and woodlands. There is no such thing as the "Upper Sonoran Desert," though the phrase is often heard.)

Lower Colorado River Valley: The subdivision of the Sonoran Desert surrounding the lower course of the Colorado River, characterized by low elevations, high temperatures, extreme aridity, primarily winter rainfall, and relatively sparse vegetation.

Mammal: A member of a group (class) of *vertebrates*, most of which have hair or fur, bear live young, and nurse them. Rodents, rabbits, javelina, deer, cats, whales, and people are all mammals.

Mesa: A flat-topped and steep-sided hill or mountain, with a width much greater than its height. Compare *butte*.

Metabolic water—see *oxidation water*

Metamorphosis: The changes some animals experience as they grow, for example the transformation of a butterfly from egg to larva, pupa, and adult. Also, the processes by which metamorphic rocks are created.

Microhabitat: The environmental conditions immediately surrounding a living thing. For example, a canyon treefrog's *habitat* is usually a rocky stream, but its typical daytime microhabitat is a smooth, nearly vertical rock surface a hop or two from the water.

Mimicry: The resemblance of one living thing to another, evolved with a biological function, such as confusing predators or prey. For example, a harmless insect may evolve a resemblance to a poisonous one and thereby gain protection from a predatory bird.

Monsoon: (mon-SOON) A seasonal shift in the direction of the prevailing winds, that brings in moist air from the sea and leads to a dramatic increase in rainfall. Or, less technically, the season in which this wind shift occurs. In the American Southwest, the monsoon imports moist tropical air chiefly from the Gulf of California, and causes the summer rainy season. (It's incorrect to call a thunderstorm a "monsoon.")

Mutualism: A close and mutually beneficial relationship between two living things, for example, the relationship between a wildflower and the bee that pollinates it. Mutualism is one of several forms of *symbiosis*.

Mycoplasma: (my-ko-PLAZ-muh) An unusual kind of bacterium that lacks a cell wall and therefore varies greatly in shape. Because many mycoplasmas are very tiny, they are poorly known, but they may infect the tissues of many animals. One species sometimes causes serious upper respiratory disease in desert tortoises.

Natural selection: Differing success among living things in producing offspring, as a result of variations in their characteristics. Natural selection is the mechanism driving *adaptation*. For example, in a population of grasshoppers those best camouflaged are most likely to mature and produce young. If their coloration is genetically inherited, the next generation will be equally or better camouflaged.

Niche: (nitch) The ecological role of a living thing. A living thing's niche includes all facets of its relationship to its *ecosystem*, including, for example, how it acquires energy, where it lives, and how it competes or cooperates with other living things. (Niche is often confused with *microhabitat*.)

Nocturnal: Active at night. Compare *diurnal* and *crepuscular*.

Nurse plant: A plant that provides a *microhabitat* suitable for the early growth of another plant. For example, saguaro seedlings are more likely to survive under the protective canopy of a nurse tree like a paloverde.

Omnivore: A living thing that eats both plants and other animals. Compare *carnivore* and *herbivore*.

Oxidation water: Water naturally produced in the body of a living thing in the process of burning (oxidizing) its food. Also called "metabolic water," it can be an important part of the water budget of a desert animal.

Ozone: A form of oxygen (O_3) that's irritating to the eyes and lungs when it occurs at ground level, but has beneficial effects when it occurs higher in the atmosphere. See *ozone layer*.

Ozone layer: A part of the *stratosphere* that contains naturally occurring ozone. The ozone layer absorbs harmful *ultraviolet* light from the sun, preventing much of it from reaching the ground.

Paleoecologist: (pay-lee-o-i-KOL-uh-jist) A scientist who studies ancient *ecosystems*.

Parasitism: (PAR-uh-site-iz-um or PAR-uh-sit-iz-um) A relationship between two living things in which one lives on or in the other, gains sustenance from it, and harms it in the process. For example, a tick on a deer's skin is a parasite. Parasitism is a form of *symbiosis*.

Parotoid glands: (puh-RO-toyd) A pair of poison glands in the skin of toads and some other *amphibians*, located behind the eyes.

Perennial plant: A plant that lives for more than two growing seasons. Compare *annual plant, biennial plant.*

Perennial stream: A stream that flows year-round.

Parthenogenesis: (par-thuh-no-JEN-uh-sis) Reproduction by a female without fertilization by a male.

pH: A measure of acidity and alkalinity. Pure water, considered to be neutral, is pH 7. Acid substances, which tend to taste sour, have pH less than 7. Alkaline (also called basic) substances, which tend to taste bitter, have pH greater than 7.

Photosynthesis: The process in which plants and certain microorganisms capture energy from visible light and convert it into stored food energy. Breathable oxygen is a byproduct of plant photosynthesis.

Pheromone: (FER-uh-mone) A chemical given off by one animal that serves as a signal to another. For example, a female moth may emit a pheromone indicating to males her location and readiness to mate.

Playa: (PLY-uh) The flat, salty floor of an undrained desert basin that sometimes becomes a shallow lake.

Pleistocene period: (PLY-stuh-seen) The period beginning roughly two million years ago, characterized by climatic shifts between cool intervals (ice ages or glacials, during which continental ice sheets formed at higher latitudes) and warm intervals (interglacials). The Pleistocene ended eleven thousand years ago, but the present warm phase (the Holocene or Recent period) may be merely another interglacial.

Pollen: Dustlike spores produced by the male reproductive parts of a seed-bearing plant, necessary for fertilization of the seeds.

Pollination: In flowering plants, the transfer of *pollen* from the male part (stamen) of a flower to the female part (pistil) of the same or another flower, frequently by wind or animals—especially insects, birds, and bats. (In pines, firs, and their relatives, pollen transfer is between male and female cones.) If the receiving plant is compatible, fertilization results, leading to the production of seeds.

Population: The collection of living things of the same species living in a given area. Examples: the saguaro population in Saguaro National Monument; the desert tortoise population east of the Colorado River.

Precocial: (pri-KO-shul) Alert, well-developed, and mobile almost immediately after hatching or birth. Examples: ducklings, fawns. Compare *altricial.*

Radiocarbon dating: Determining the age of plant or animal remains by measuring the amount of carbon-14 they contain. Since carbon-14 breaks down (decays radioactively) at a known rate, the amount remaining allows an estimation of the time since death.

Rain shadow: A region on the downwind side of a mountain range that is relatively arid because moisture has been removed from the air by precipitation over the mountains.

Raptor: A bird of prey, such as a hawk or an owl.

Rayleigh scattering: *Scattering* of light (or other electromagnetic radiation) by very tiny particles (much smaller than its wavelength). Visible sunlight from the blue end of the spectrum is most strongly scattered by air molecules, causing the sky to appear blue. (Invisible *ultraviolet* light is more strongly scattered still, making it possible to receive a sunburn from exposure to the sky even when shaded from the sun.)

Reptile: A member of the group (class) of *vertebrates* that includes turtles, crocodiles, lizards, and snakes. Reptiles are typically cold-blooded air breathers with scaly skins, and most lay eggs. Compare *amphibian.*

Riparian: (ruh-PARE-ee-un or ry-PAIR-ee-un) Having to do with the bank or shore of a lake, river, or stream. In the Sonoran Desert, riparian communities are very important centers of *biodiversity.*

Scavenger: An animal that habitually feeds on the dead remains of other animals (carrion).

Scattering: In physics, the bouncing of moving particles off other small objects, for example the bouncing of light particles (photons) off dust in the atmosphere. See also *Rayleigh scattering.*

Sediment: A material such as clay, silt, sand, or gravel, composed of fragments usually created by the *erosion* of rocks, and transported and deposited by gravity, water, ice, or wind.

Sonora: (so-NO-ruh) A state in northern Mexico, immediately south of Arizona.

Sonoran Desert: A warm North American desert comprising much of the state of Sonora, as well as southwestern Arizona, southeastern California, and most of Baja California.

Species: A *population* of living things that interbreed freely and produce fertile offspring, and are reproductively isolated from other such populations. Because they exchange genes in the process of interbreeding, members of a species tend to be similar in genetic make-up and appearance.

Stratosphere: The clear, stable, and nearly weatherless layer of the atmosphere above the level of most clouds. Commercial jetliners cruise in the stratosphere.

Subsidence: (sub-SIDE-ens or SUB-si-dens) Settling or sinking of the land's surface, such as caused by withdrawal of ground water and compacting of the remaining sediments.

Succulent plant: A plant that stores moisture in thickened stems, leaves, or roots, for example, a cactus or an agave.

Symbiosis: (sim-by-O-sis or sim-bee-O-sis) A close relationship of dependence between two living things in which one or both benefit. Ecologists recognize three basic forms of symbiosis: see *commensalism, mutualism,* and *parasitism.*

Territory: An area defended by an animal against others of the same or different species. A territory may be part or all of an animal's *home range*.

Thornscrub: A *biotic community* transitional between desert and tropical forest, in which the vegetation is dominated by thorny, *drought deciduous* trees and shrubs.

Tinaja: (tee-NA-ha) A Spanish word for a natural stone depression, usually scoured by an intermittent stream, that sometimes holds water. Also called "tanks," tinajas are important water sources for some desert wildlife.

Transpiration: The loss of water by evaporation from plant surfaces. Most plants transpire chiefly through their leaves.

Trichomoniasis: (trik-uh-muh-NY-uh-sis) Any disease caused by a microorganism (protozoan) in the genus *Trichomonas*. Trichomoniasis is sometimes serious in some birds, including doves, pigeons, and certain hawks, and can be spread at birdbaths and feeders.

Ultraviolet: An invisible form of radiation beyond the violet end of the visible spectrum. UV rays are more energetic than visible light, and are capable of causing sunburn and skin cancer, as well as damage to man-made substances like plastics and dyes.

UV—see *ultraviolet*

Venom: A poison produced by an animal and delivered by injection, typically through a bite or sting. (Therefore, a rattlesnake is a venomous animal, but a toad, though poisonous, is not.)

Valley fever—see *coccidioidomycosis*

Vertebrate: An animal with a backbone or spine. Fishes, amphibians, reptiles, birds, and mammals are all vertebrates. Compare *invertebrate*.

Vestigial organ: (ve-STIJ-ee-ul or ve-STIJ-ul) An imperfectly developed organ in a living thing, derived from an organ more completely developed in an evolutionary ancestor. For example, our appendix is a vestige of a branch (the caecum) in the digestive system of a distant ancestor of humans.

Virga: (VUR-guh) Wisps of rain that evaporate before reaching the ground.

Wash: A (frequently sandy-floored) streambed that's usually dry and has sloping banks. Compare *arroyo*.

Water table: The upper limit of an *aquifer*; the level that must be reached by a water well.

Xeriscape: (ZEER-i-scape) A low water use artificial landscape, such as a garden planted with desert species.

Zoonotic disease: (zo-uh-NOT-ic) A disease that can be passed from animals to humans. Also called a "zoonosis" (zo-ON-uh-sis or zo-uh-NO-sis).

INDEX

Sonoran Desert toad, 106-108
sotol, 21-22
spadefoot toads, 29-31, **29, 30**
Spaniards, 38, 40
spring, 12
spurges, 22
squirrels, **13, 51**, 52, 53
subsidence, land, 37
succulent plants, 20, 22, 45
sunburn, 27, 46, 95
sunsets, 15-17
surface water, 35-37

tarantulas, 114
teddy bear cholla, 25, 100-102, **102**
thunderstorms, 12-13, 17, 94, 122
tinajas, 40, 105
toads, 29-31, 106-108
Tohono O'odham, 13, 39
tortoise adoption program, 109-110
trichomoniasis, 59-61

ultraviolet light (UV), 27, 95
upper respiratory tract disease (URTD), 111

valley fever (cocci), 117-119, 122
venomous animals, 65-75, 76, 79-81, 112-116
visible spectrum, 15-16

washes, 35, 36, 104-105, 121-122
water
    emergency sources, 97-99
    requirements of desert plants, 43-45
    requirements while hiking, 95
    sources for Native Americans, 38-40
    sources for urban areas, 35-37
    sources for wildlife, 104-105
water holes
    in gardens, 51, 54
    natural, 40, 105, 124
water table, 35-37
whipsnakes, 77-78, 77
whiptail lizards, 24, **24**
wildfire, 28, 110-111
wildlife in gardens and yards
    attracting, 53-58

    caring for injured, sick, or orphaned, 62-64
    dangerous species, 65-75, 76, 79-81, 87-88
    diseases of, 59-61
    preventing damage by, 44, 51-52, 82-83
    preventing injury to, 56, 60, 88
wildlife in natural habitats
    dangerous species, 106-107, 112-116
    finding and viewing, 103-105
    preventing disturbance to, 121, 124
wildlife rehabilitator, licensed, 62
winter, 13-14, 47
woodpeckers, 82-83
woodrats, 84-86

yuccas, 21, **21**

ABOUT THE AUTHOR

Naturalist David Wentworth Lazaroff divides his time among writing, photography, and natural science education in Tucson elementary schools. His fascination with the Santa Catalina Mountains outside Tucson resulted in the publication of *Sabino Canyon: The Life of a Southwestern Oasis* (University of Arizona Press), which was voted one of the "Best Southwestern Books of 1993" by the *Arizona Daily Star*. He is also the author of the Arizona-Sonora Desert Museum's popular book *The Secret Lives of Hummingbirds*.

David regrets that he's unable to answer the perennial Sonoran Desert question, "Can you really fry an egg on the hood of your car in July?" He drives a Volkswagen bus.